Fruit Desserts!
by Dorothy Parker

Edited by Andrea Chesman

The Crossing Press, Freedom, California 95019

Printed in the U.S.A. by McNaughton & Gunn, Ann Arbor, Mi.

Library of Congress-in-Publication Data

Parker, Dorothy, 1922-
    Fruit desserts

    (The Crossing Press specialty cookbook series)
    Includes index
    1. Desserts. 2. Cookery (Fruit) I. Chesman, Andrea
II. Title. III. Series
TX773.P295 1987   641.8'6   87-6666
ISBN 0-89594-226-7
ISBN 0-89594-225-9 (pbk.)

Contents

Introduction 5

Fruit Savvy 9

Quick No-Cook Concoctions 25

Quick Custards, Molds, and Fools 41

Fruit Puddings and Souffles 57

Tarts, Pies, Crumbles, and Cobblers 71

Cakes and Bars 101

Frosty Delights 119

Miscellany and Exotica 149

Index 167

INTRODUCTION

Fruit . . . few words equal this one in resonance and the power to conjure up tastes, images, memories—of fragrances, of sights, of seasons, of pleasures and delights beheld and consumed. Small wonder that a fruit was the product of the Tree of Knowledge.

In the world of food it is often the case that what tastes good is bad for you. What is amazing is that as luscious, as sweet and succulent, as deeply gratifying, as aromatic and florally fragrant as they are, fruits of every variety are healthfully good for you, bursting with nutrients, fortified with fiber—unlike desserts loaded with sugar. The recipes in this book capitalize on the natural sweetness of various fruits and keep the addition of sugar to a minimum.

When you add to the obvious virtues of fresh fruits their versatility and adaptability, it is impossible to contest the assertion that here is the ideal food. Moreover, as the reaction against sugar-filled junk food has become more widespread, as con-sciousness of weight control and good health has deepened, so too has a new appreciation of the benefits of fresh fruits and vegetables grown, and with it an increasing awareness that the whole world has become the fruit-lover's domain.

Until recently we found a rather narrow assortment of fruits in local markets, and a not much wider one in expensive specialty shops. Now, as American palates have become more sophisticated, the demand has grown for formerly rare and exotic fruits from other regions of the world—Asia, Africa, the Middle East, the Caribbean, Latin America—and they have become commonplace in neighborhood produce shops. It's a very poor and unimaginative supermarket indeed—or an uninformed fruit buyer—that does not routinely stock kiwi, mango, guava, papaya, and passion fruit these days.

This book presents a number of ways of preparing and serving fruits. Many of the recipes are followed by variations, so you can adapt the recipes to other fruit you may have on hand. But beyond what's covered here, the ways are virtually infinite; the only limiting factor is the imagination of the cook or hostess. Once the habit of fruit desserts is formed, once the world of fruit has been assimilated into your style and perspective, you'll find there's no going back, nor any wish to. For my part, I can do nicely without meat; but I can't go a day without fruit. And more and more of us are coming to share this view. Welcome to the garden of earthly delights!

A Note About Sugar

Although specific amounts of sugar appear in the ingredients lists, the recipes in this book should be read with a qualification in mind: Use more or less, depending on the sweetness of the fruit. Rely on your taste buds and knowledge of the fruit you're working with to make this adjustment. Except for the recipes in chapter 5 (Cakes and Bars), where bulk and texture may be affected by a change in the sugar measurement, this advice applies to every recipe in the book. Remember, numbers can be wrong; your senses are not.

The same admonition applies to other sweeteners, such as honey, maple syrup, molasses, corn syrup: The amount should be scaled down with a very sweet fruit, or it can be increased judiciously for a fruit with less than optimum sweetness and flavor. Bear in mind that if you substitute one of these sweeteners for the sugar in one of these recipes, you will need less of it than you would need of sugar.

1
FRUIT SAVVY

If you feel as I do about fruit, you save its selection until everything else is already in your shopping cart, keeping the best until last. This highly personal quest doesn't at all resemble the acquisition of most other foods, including those that require judicious comparison and contrast and ordinary good judgment. Delicate discrimination is called for. I often think that the selection is comparable to that governing a work of art; and I try, and urge others to try, to bring to it the deliberation they might employ in selecting for purchase a painting or a work of sculpture. The composition these beautiful objects will make in the wooden bowl on my kitchen counter is never far from my mind when I'm marketing for fruit.

If you can buy locally grown fruit, you're in luck; the peaches ripened on the tree in the orchard across town, the berries picked from the farm or berry patch down the road a piece quite simply taste better. Most fruit from far away has been picked before it is fully mature, and unripe fruit has not developed its full flavor. Nor will it as it makes its way to your table.

The refrigerator is a proper storage place for most fruits only after they have achieved perfect ripeness, and then only if you don't plan to use them that very day. If you do refrigerate them, remember to remove them from the refrigerator and leave them at room temperature for a few hours before eating or cooking them. This is a way to enhance juiciness and flavor.

Your produce shop or supermarket may include a "marked-down" or "day-old" shelf; check it out every time you go there. Occasionally some fruit is placed there at the very summit of its ripeness and desirability, for no better reason than to make room for an incoming shipment. Sometimes you can get firm, unblemished apples, pears, or peaches; berries that have not even begun to dry out; fragrant melons with no bruises or soft spots — at significant savings, or even at giveaway prices. These are exceptions, of course; as a rule, for fresh fruits to serve with little or no cooking, you are better advised to concentrate on the regular produce department. Examine your finds carefully for texture; firmness; unbroken, unblemished skins; appropriate color, shape, heft, size, fragrance—and reject those that don't please you in all these respects.

About Fruits

In the pages that follow are some specific notions about specific fruits: when they are in season, how to choose the best fruit, where and how to store them, and ways to recognize ideal ripeness. There are also some suggestions as to the best ways to use different fruits and turn them into seductive desserts.

Apples. Possibly the most versatile of fruits, the apple grows in hundreds of varieties all over the United States. Their peak season depends on the variety and location, and can vary from September to October for McIntosh to November through April for Baldwin and Winesap. On the whole, autumn is the best time for fresh apples; the rest of the year most of us have to make do with apples from commercial storage.

This may come as a surprise to admirers of McIntosh and Rome Beauty and Northern Spy (some of the best eating apples in the Northeast), but there are more Red Delicious grown in the U.S. than any other apple. Jonathan, Winesap, Gravenstein, and Macoun are firmly textured and richly flavorful; they are just as good for eating raw as for cooking. Cortlands are ideal for make-ahead fruit cups and such because their sweet, snow-white flesh resists darkening when exposed to air. Grimes Golden, Rhode Island Greening, and Golden Delicious are among the non-red apples that are pleasing both raw and cooked.

Buy only as many apples as you can comfortably cook or eat within a couple of weeks—unless you come upon a bargain in "windfalls" or "drops," which are perfect for applesauce, pies, sorbets, cakes. And in summertime, when you're anticipating the autumn apple crop, you may be able to get Granny Smiths, which with their thick green skins and lovely succulence, travel well and are fine eaters and cookers. Many of them are imported; the Granny Smiths in my supermarket in summer come from the South of France.

Apricots. A fresh, ripe apricot is a wondrous thing to behold: firm, round, plump, the color of the sun. Its peak season is June and July. Most U.S. apricots are grown in California, from which they are almost never shipped ripe. But the dried version is delicious, too, and very useful for cooked desserts such as pies, cakes, puddings.

Avocados. The handsome, pear-shaped avocado grows all year-round in tropical climes, and it is usually shipped hard and unripe to other parts of the world. Ripen it at home at room temperature. When per-fect for eating, its smooth or nubby skin is either bright green or greenish-black, its flesh firm, not soft, with a little give at the stem end. The rather bland, buttery, slightly nutty taste of avocado makes it just right for a hundred desserts, from pudding to mousse to ice cream. Slice it, cut it in chunks, or puree it, and enjoy it by itself or as "background" for other, more assertively flavored fruits.

Bananas. Although they don't grow in any of the United States, there's hardly a produce shop from supermarket to the tiniest delicatessen that does not have bananas constantly in stock. According to some polls, it is the fruit most favored by Americans of all ages.

The banana is shipped from Latin America year-round. Ideally ripe, it has black spots or streaks in its golden peel; it is perfect then for eating fresh or mashing. But if you buy bananas yellow-green, there is no problem with ripening them—at room temperature it will happen almost too quickly. When over-ripe, the banana is great for cakes and other baked desserts.

Despite the admonition of Chiquita, you *can* put (whole) bananas in the refrigerator; the skins will darken, but the fruit inside will keep fresh for several days.

Berries. The berrying season stretches from late spring to early winter, and so many kinds are so often free for the picking that it's almost a shame to have to buy them. Blueberries, raspberries, mulberries, and blackberries—those that you can manage not to eat as you pick them—make wonderful toppings and fillings for all kinds of puddings, pies, and cakes. They have a natural affinity for cream (sour, whipped, or poured from a pitcher). Cranberries, currants, and gooseberries, too sour or tart for eating out of hand, take kindly to sweetening and slight cooking, after which they glorify fools, mousses, sorbets, molds, and ice creams.

In this book, for simplicity's sake, the general term blackberry subsumes many varieties, such as dewberry, loganberry, and boysenberry. Blueberry takes in huckleberry, bilberry, and the amusingly named whortleberry. Cranberry includes its relative lingonberry. But the beautiful gooseberry is in a class by itself, varying in size from blueberry to cherry tomato, and in color from white to green to deep purple.

If you can't examine berries one by one when you buy them, be sure those you can see are plump and unbroken, and that their container is not leaking juice. Store them in the refrigerator. Or freeze them in plastic bags—one of the advantages of this method of storage is that you can defrost them a few at a time, to eat as they are, add to a fruit cup, or use as a garnish.

Carambolas. The unusual-looking tropical carambola, now being grown successfully in Florida, is best bought from August through February. Its pale orange, rather waxy flesh and five-finned shape make it a natural for slicing crosswise into decorative stars (star fruit is another name for it).

Carambola's acid, citrusy flavor can vary from flowery-sweet to sour, and knowing which you're buying is something of a puzzle. Narrow ribs suggest tartness; plump fleshiness, the sweeter variety. Select full, firm fruits (a brown edge to the ribs is okay; it may even promise a sweeter fruit). If you don't eat them at once, store them at room temperature—or in the refrigerator, where they will keep for about two weeks.

Combine carambolas with blander fruits, use the slices for a garnish for sherbets and custards—or eat the fruit by itself in superb splendor—simply slice and serve on a dessert plate.

Cherries. Sour cherries have a shorter season—June to mid-August—than sweet, which are picked from May through September. Perfect ripeness is characterized by firm plumpness and intense bright color, which, depending on the variety, ranges from purple-maroon through all shades of red to salmon-pink.

Cherries are marvelously adaptable, performing well in a whole range of frozen, jellied, and cooked desserts. They combine well with sour cream, yogurt, and cottage cheese. And, of course, what summer treat is so rare as picking cherries from the tree and eating them from your hand?

If you lack a cherry pitter, try getting those pesky pits out with the tip of a vegetable peeler, or even one round end of a paper clip.

Citrus Fruits. Most citrus fruits are grown in southern climes year-round, although some varieties of orange, such as navel, temple, and blood, have a peak season from fall through spring. Whether you're buying oranges and grapefruits for eating fresh, or lemons and limes for garnishes and juice, choose plump, heavy, firm fruits with fine-textured skin, and sniff them for clean, astringent fragrance.

November is the peak month for tangerines, tangelos, and mandarin oranges (actually a variety of tangerine), although they can be found from October through February. Their firm sections and glorious color make them an excellent choice for topping cheesecakes and ice creams, and mixing with other fruits in parfaits, fruit cups, sorbets. (Speaking of color, don't be surprised if the much-prized pink grapefruit loses its color after being cut open or squeezed for juice. The Florida Burgundy, however, is one variety that will hold its blush, even unto grapefruit juice.)

Oranges and grapefruit, cut up or sectioned, blend happily into flans, sherbets, mousses, and other cool concoctions. And how unthinkable life would be without the piquant flavor of lemon or lime juice to accent the taste of other fruits before using them in tarts, cobblers, crisps, whips, creams, and molds!

Store citrus fruits in the refrigerator, but always leave them at room temperature for a few hours before eating or cooking with them. (A lemon or lime wrapped in foil or plastic and refrigerated will stay fresh and juicy a very long time.) And before peeling or cutting any citrus fruit, roll it along a hard surface a few times to release optimum flavor and succulence.

Figs. From June to October in California you can pick or buy these plump, fragrant fruits and eat them as they are, or in combination with other less assertively flavored fruits. Like the apricot, the fig does not take kindly to shipping fresh, and over-ripe (a condition it reaches quickly) it acquires a sour smell. If you've never eaten a fresh fig, there's a treat in store for you—simply slice it and eat it with a fork. Dried figs, with which most of us must make do, are fine enhancements for puddings, cakes, and pies.

Grapes. Depending on the variety—and what a wonderful, bountiful range of types and colors they come in!—United States table grapes are in season from May through November, with a high period of September-October, although some California varieties ripen from November through May.

The deep purple end of the spectrum is best represented in the East by the Concord grape, which matures in September and October. But Easterners have not lived who have never experienced the large purple Ribier grape, shipped from California, as is the purple Fredonia, all through the fall.

Among red grapes, California provides us with the Tokay, Emperor, Malaga, and Cardinal. The best Eastern red table grape may be the Delaware, or the maroon-colored Catawba.

The green grape category comprises fruit in delicate shades of ivory, gold, yellow, and pale green. In the East, this group is most notably represented by the Golden Niagara; in the South by the Muscadine; and California by the Almeria and the incomparable Thompson Seedless.

Oddly enough, most thin-skinned, seedless grapes are located in the white-green classification, while all black-purple grapes are thick-skinned and heavily seeded, with the red group occupying the middle ground as to seed number and skin thickness.

Whatever the color, size, or shape, choose plump, unshriveled grapes still firmly attached to stems. Refrigerate them if you're not using them within twenty-four hours. Eat grapes by popping them into your mouth one by one, or in combination with other fruits (three colors of grapes with diced apples and kiwis and fresh mint leaves make a comely, tasty fruit cup), or in chilled concoctions. And by all means use them for garnishes.

Guavas. This small, oval, many-seeded tropical fruit is available year-round in California and the deep South; its peak season is from June to September. Choose guavas that are firm but not hard, and let them soften at room temperature. Guava skin color ranges from pale yellow to yellow-green, the flesh inside from white to yellow to red. Its aroma, unpleasant and animal-like when green, turns fruitily pleasant as it ripens. And its taste is reminiscent of strawberry, pineapple, or banana—or all three.

Guava is good to eat raw—just halve it and spoon the flesh out of the skin—but perhaps even better cut in chunks or pureed for baked desserts, or chilled and frozen ones. Remove the skin (peel as thinly as you can) or leave it on (in some varieties the skin is edible). Whether to seed the fruit or not depends on the variety, some having coarser seeds than others.

Kiwis. The kiwi's subtle sweet-tart flavor (somewhere between that of a melon and a strawberry) and the startling jewel-green hue of its flesh, with white core and black (edible) seed corolla, make eating this fruit a fascinating experience the first time encountered. Kiwifruit is shipped from New Zealand from October through May; it is available domestically from June through November. Growers pick the kiwi unripe, and its hardness, together with its tough brown hairy skin (from which it gets its name, shared with a New Zealand bird) makes it an ideal fruit to ship.

Select firm fruits, a little under-ripe, and let them ripen—soften a little—at room temperature, or in a paper bag with a banana enclosed. A perfectly ripe kiwifruit feels like a not-quite-tender peach. Eat the peeled slices by themselves or with other raw fruits or berries. Include sliced kiwi in a fruit cup of fresh pineapple, cherries, bananas, apples, and grapes. Or puree it and put it into a mousse or a custard.

Kumquats. The peak season for kumquats, grown in this country in small quantities in California and Florida, is winter. They look like tiny, football-shaped, yellow-skinned oranges, and the flavor of the flesh—a sort of concentrated tart orange taste—contrasts oddly with the sweetness of the skin. Select firm-skinned fruit and store them in the refrigerator until you're ready to use them as fresh-fruit contrasts with blander fruits, or pureed for baked desserts. Kumquats can be eaten whole, out of hand—but it is an acquired taste.

Mangoes. Imported mangoes are available from January through October, but the domestic varieties, mostly from Florida, are at their peak June through August. This round or oval-shaped, thick-skinned fruit, more nearly ubiquitous in over half the world than the apple, comes in three sizes, the smallest like a small apple, the largest sometimes tipping the scales at three pounds each.

Choose fruit that is only partly ripe, its light green skin showing some yellow or red, its smooth exterior firm and taut. With the mango use your nose—sniff the stem end for a pleasant fragrance rather like that of pine trees wafted on an evening breeze. Ripen the fruit at room temperature, and use it before it becomes soft or flabby. Its subtle flavor varies with the variety, and to some palates is reminiscent of fresh peach or pineapple. Some mangoes are filled with nectar that makes a refreshing drink.

Eat mango fresh, cut in chunks, alone or combined with other fruits; or add it to puddings, pies, cakes, or chilled or frozen desserts. The flesh of the mango is not obliging—it doesn't fall away easily and conveniently; it holds fast to both skin and stone. The mango will test your patience and try your skills. When no one else is looking on, you can take the relatively easy way out by turning the half inside out and in a lovely, messy way burying your face in it and having at it—and wash away the evidence later. But when you're trying to retrieve the flesh in order to employ it in a dessert, be patient, be cautious, breathe deeply and evenly at all times—and use a sharp knife.

Melons. In this country, the peak season for cantaloupe is March through December; for Casaba, August through November; for honeydew, June through October; and for watermelon, June through September. The nose test for ripeness, plus slight give when you press it at the blossom end, works for cantaloupe, Casaba, and honeydew. But for watermelon it's a tap test — it should make a hollow sound when you thump it.

Any kind of melon — lucky the food shopper who is offered a choice of some of the rarer varieties such as Charentais, Spanish, Persian, Crenshaw, Honeyball — is a good choice when you are looking for a fruit that requires little preparation. Melons are also wonderfully refreshing in frozen sorbets, molds, mousses, sherbets, and ice creams. Berries combine with melons well, offering flavor and color contrasts, such as raspberry with honeydew, blueberry with cantaloupe, blackberry with Casaba.

Papayas. This delicately floral-tasting tropical fruit — not to be confused with the fruit of the temperate-climate pawpaw tree — is grown year-round in Hawaii, Florida, and the West Coast. It is shipped while still green and will ripen in a few days at room temperature, sealed in a paper bag with a banana. In the U.S. we see papayas that are either round or pear-shaped (though some varieties are shaped like bananas or huge pecans). Choose fruit that is at least partly yellow (or orange or rose, depending on the variety) and soft but not mushy. Never chill papaya until it is fully ripe.

Raw, a papaya can be sprinkled with lime juice and eaten by itself from the skin. Papaya also combines well with more sharply flavored fruits, such as grapefruit, orange, strawberry, pineapple. Or use it as the basis of mousses, sherbets, ice creams.

Halved, the papaya reveals a central cavity full to bursting with edible gray-black seeds in a gelatinous coating — they taste like nothing, unless it's peppery watercress. Papaya seeds, toasted and lightly salted, can be used as garnishes or eaten from the hand, like peanuts.

Passion Fruit. The first time you try passion fruit, just halve it crosswise and eat its golden-orange flesh, seeds and all, with a spoon. If it's too tart, sweeten it with a little honey. This tropical fruit, grown year-round in Florida, keeps very well—at room temperature, in the refrigerator, or you can freeze it (which breaks down the very firm pulp, rendering it easier to puree). When perfectly ripe, it has a purplish-black wrinkled skin and sounds sloshy when shaken. If by chance you should find yourself in possession of a round passion fruit with a smooth, unbroken skin, ripen it at room temperature for a few days.

Peaches and Nectarines. From May through October, U.S. peach growers keep us supplied with this most delicious and versatile fruit. In the market choose firm but not hard fruit of good yellow color with blushes of red or orange. If you find some not quite ripe, wrap them in tissue paper and leave them at room temperature for up to a week. Eat them raw, or use them in gelatins, mousses, puddings, pastries, cakes, ice creams, sherbets, and sorbets. All of this counsel applies equally to nectarines, with the added advantage that you needn't peel them.

Pears. In October and November, big pears like the roundish, chartreuse Comice, the brownish-yellow Bosc and Anjou (or the Red Anjou), and the yellow-green Bartlett are at the peak of their seasons, although some of these varieties are grown right through to May. Clapp Favorite, a sweet, smooth, juicy pear, is in season from August through November. Other good Eastern pears, which mature mostly from September through November, are Tyson, Gorham, Seckel, Cayuga, and

Winter Nelis. The roundish, golden-skinned, wonderfully succulent Asian pear grows in warm parts of the country from August through February.

No matter what the variety, buy pears that are firm but not hard, as ripening at home (individually tissue-wrapped, at room temperature) is tricky since they leap from unripe to over-ripe so speedily.

There's no treat quite like a sweet, juicy pear picked from the tree and eaten on the spot. But pears combine beautifully with other fruits and berries; and they lend themselves felicitously to poaching, and to mousses, cakes, sherbets, ice creams. They are even great in pies and tarts—instead of pumpkin pie after your next Thanksgiving dinner, serve a Blackberry Pear Tart and collect paeans from your family and guests.

Persimmons. The native American persimmon at the peak of ripeness is a thing of great beauty: its delicate flame-orange skin gleaming like ceramic, its acorn or tomato form crowned with an exquisitely modeled greenish-brown calyx. It is found in markets from October through February, too often either hard and unripe or over-ripe and mushy. Its domestic provenance is California; but exotic varieties come to us from Latin America, North Africa, and Southern Europe.

Perfectly ripe, a persimmon is plump and tender-soft; careful peeling of the thin skin reveals a luscious treat to be eaten fresh. It has a subtle flavor that may remind you of plums and honey. Unripe persimmons (puckery-tart and inedible) can be ripened in a paper bag with a banana enclosed, at room temperature.

A ripe persimmon half, in its skin, sprinkled with brown sugar and broiled for half a minute, makes a delectable dessert. Persimmon also combines well with other subtly flavored fruits. Its flesh, pressed through a coarse sieve, can provide the basis of a pudding or a cake.

Pineapples. Available year-round from the tropics, fresh pineapple is more versatile than many cooks realize. Eat it raw in combination with other fruits; soften it and add it to puddings, pies, cakes, ice creams. Its woody texture and excessive tartness tends to set the teeth on edge; but these qualities can be tamed somewhat by marinating the fruit in wine or simmering for a few minutes in water (or using the canned fruit).

If you do buy pineapple fresh, use the nose test — it should be assertively fragrant — and choose heavy fruit with flat "eyes." The only cautionary note about fresh pineapple that needs stating is to avoid combining it with gelatin; an enzyme it contains prevents thickening — a sort of natural anticoagulant.

Plums and Prunes. The season for domestic plums of European derivation is June and July, while those Asian varieties grown on the West Coast are available from August through October. Buy them plump and soft enough to yield a bit to touch and slightly puckered around the stem. Fresh plums eaten out of hand are a late summer to early autumn joy; they also give pleasure in mousses, puddings, fools, cakes, and tarts. Keep plums in plastic bags in the refrigerator until shortly before you're ready to turn them into luscious desserts.

Dried as prunes, they are one of the easiest fruits to store in the cupboard. Refresh prunes in water, ginger ale, or wine, a few at a time; or put them without soaking into cakes, bars, and cobblers.

Quinces. Although the quince blossom is one of the loveliest in nature, the fragrant fruit cannot be eaten raw. Its hard ivory flesh, cooked slowly, turns orange, develops a rich flavor, and lends itself well to stewing or pureeing and adding to cakes, puddings, and frozen desserts. (For amplifying the flavor of pears, apples, mangoes, and papayas, add to them a few slices of quince that has been peeled and simmered in water for ten to fifteen minutes).

Quinces grow all over the continental

United States. Most varieties produce fruit from September to November.

Rhubarb. Another plant that we don't eat raw, rhubarb develops its stiff red stalks in the garden or hothouse in most of the fifty states any time between February and August, depending on the climate. Cooked with sugar or honey, rhubarb is quickly converted into a lovely sauce to eat by itself or use in molds, cakes, and chilled or frozen desserts. Rhubarb is at its peak during strawberry season; the two together make an incomparable pie. (In fact, rhubarb is known as pie plant in some localities—and was once called wine plant in others.)

Caution: the foliage and roots of rhubarb are toxic. So trim off all the green leaves and white root portions carefully, leaving only the succulent red or green stalks, before you cut them up for cooking.

Strawberries. You will find the aristocratic strawberry growing somewhere in the U.S. all year-round; but it is most plentiful from May through August. At the market, select solid, well-shaped fruits with hulls attached; reject those in leaky boxes. Eat them fresh or cook them as soon as possible after picking as they start losing their flavor within a few hours. Given a huge quantity, freeze some whole strawberries in strawberry sauce in a liquid-tight container. (Make the sauce by crushing strawberries in a little white wine with a little sugar added.)

A few crushed strawberries can do much to enhance the flavor and color of some dishes more pallid in taste and hue, such as applesauce, pureed pears, or mango or papaya pudding. There is no type of dessert in this book that the strawberry won't grace—but there is also nothing quite as close to ambrosia as a dish of sweet, ripe, juicy strawberries in a little cream.

Post Scripts

Many fruits (and some nuts) can be peeled more easily by plunging them for a few seconds into very hot water, just off the boil, followed by a few seconds in cold water. Try this with apples, apricots, kiwis, peaches, and plums.

Having peeled a fruit that you don't want to turn brown or otherwise discolor, dip it, whole, halved, or sliced, in the juice of a lemon or other citrus fruit. This treatment is recommended for apples, avocados, bananas, guavas, mangoes, pears, peaches, nectarines, and passion fruit.

2
QUICK NO-COOK CONCOCTIONS

The simple pleasure of sweet, fresh berries, picked in the sun and eaten out of hand, is unequaled. A slice of perfectly ripened melon consumed on the back lawn provides one of life's perfect moments. A peach or an apple, round, firm, fragrant, and succulent, right off the tree, is a radiant experience. So much we all know. But after a well-prepared, beautifully served lunch or dinner — something else is called for.

In the pages that follow are some suggestions for making fresh fruit into an event, a suitable finale to a good balanced meal — without cooking, with only a stroke of the hand, a spin or two of the blender. In much of the world this is the prevailing manner with desserts. Cultivate it!

Here are some fruit combinations you may never have thought of, some ways of serving that add a dash of elegance to an otherwise simple presentation, some notions that will stimulate your imagination into flights of fancy and improvisation.

Before moving on to the recipes, check out the following baker's dozen simple ideas for serving fresh fruit:

- Seedless green or red grapes in a goblet, stirred into sour cream or yogurt (or a combination of the two), spooned into a goblet and sprinkled with brown sugar.

- Strawberries, sprinkled with sugar and set aside for 30 minutes, then spooned over yogurt, ice cream, or pound cake.

- Honeydew or cantaloupe, halved, their cavities filled with fresh blueberries, raspberries, or blackberries.

- Pineapple, kiwi, banana, orange, or avocado slices, or whole strawberries, served with fondue forks for dipping into a fondue pot full of warm fudge sauce.

- Pears or apples, whole perfect fruits, served with wedges of spreadable cheese (such as Camembert or Brie) and dessert knives.

- Watermelon, honeydew, and cantaloupe balls, tossed in a little kirsch or fruit brandy, served in champagne glasses.

- Pineapple or mango chunks, with forks, for dipping into a cup of pure maple syrup.

- Passion fruits, halved, sprinkled with a little applejack, served with demitasse spoons.

- Banana or avocado chunks, and forks, for dipping into a cup of molasses cut with a little lemon juice.

- Peaches or nectarines, halved, their cavities mounded with cottage cheese and sprinkled with Frangelico.

- Pink grapefruit sections and avocado slices, sprinkled with a little pear brandy.

- Cherries, kumquats, small plums, and apple chunks, strung in series on kabob skewers, rolled in confectioner's sugar.

- Chunks of all your favorite fruits in a large wooden bowl, a platter of confectioner's sugar beside it, skewers distributed to diners for them to make their own selections. This one had better be at an al fresco picnic!

Carambola Stars

4 small fresh carambolas
2 medium-size apples
¼ cup grapefruit juice

Yield: 4 servings

For your first meeting with this beautiful, orange, five-ribbed fruit (sometimes called star fruit), I suggest you cut it into star-shaped slices, put them on a white platter, and just stare at them for some time. Or you might serve them this way.

Peel any brown edges that may have appeared on the carambola ribs, then cut the fruit crosswise into thin slices. Peel and halve the apples and cut into thin slices.

Cover the surface of a serving platter with the apple slices and arrange the carambola stars on top. Sprinkle the fruit with the grapefruit juice; leave it at room temperature for a few minutes before serving it.

Serve with a spatula onto dessert plates. Give a knife and fork to each diner—and wait for the expressions of delight.

Fresh Fig Ambrosia

1 large avocado
6 fresh ripe figs
12 vanilla wafers
2 tablespoons pear brandy

Yield: 4 servings

On a business trip to the West Coast, after a shattering encounter with the Los Angeles freeway, I arrived at what seemed to me at the time the Garden of Eden: in my friend's backyard both figs and avocados grew in profusion. I was served this luscious dish made from fresh-picked fruits.

Peel and slice the avocado and arrange the slices on 4 dessert plates.

Chop the figs into ½-inch pieces, taking care not to lose any of the juice. Crumble the cookies and stir the crumbs into the figs and fig juice. Distribute this mixture over the avocado slices on each plate.

Sprinkle the brandy over the figs and serve at once.

Berry Parfait

2 cups raspberries, blackberries,
   strawberries, or blueberries
½ cup plain yogurt
1 (3-ounce) package cream cheese,
   softened
1 tablespoon honey

Yield: 4 servings

Here's a quick dessert that is very rich, very sweet, and very festive.

Spoon the berries into a blender or food processor and run it at low speed for a few seconds. Set aside.

Combine the yogurt, cream cheese, and honey in the blender or food processor and blend until you have a smooth mixture. Spoon the berries and the yogurt mixture alternately into chilled parfait glasses and serve cold.

Variations

Peach Parfait. Substitute 2 cups sliced fresh peaches for the berries.

Cherry Parfait. Substitute 2 cups chopped sweet ripe cherries for the berries.

Fresh Apricot Supreme

4 to 5 fresh apricots, sliced
½ cup chopped dates
1 tangerine, peeled, seeded, sectioned
½ cup honey
½ cup shredded coconut
1 pint plain yogurt

Yield: 5 to 6 servings

Some years ago, I took keen pleasure in a lovely fresh apricot dish in Narsai David's fine enterprising restaurant in the San Francisco Bay Area. Here is my own free-wheeling version of that memorable dessert.

Mix all these ingredients together and chill the mixture for 2 or 3 hours in the refrigerator. Serve the dessert cold, in small portions—it is very rich.

Variation

Dried Apricot Supreme. Substitute 5 or 6 dried apricots for the fresh apricots. For the tangerine, substitute 1 orange, peeled, seeded, and sliced, and any juice that may escape from it in the handling.

31

Strawberry Banana Fool

1 pint fresh strawberries
4 tablespoons sugar
2 fresh ripe bananas
2 cups heavy cream
Mint sprigs

Yield: 4 to 6 servings

This whip is double the fun.

Crush the strawberries and puree them in a blender or food processor, adding 2 tablespoons of the sugar.

Puree the bananas in a blender or food processor, adding the remaining 2 tablespoons sugar.

Whip the cream until soft peaks form. Fold half the whipped cream into the strawberry puree, half into the banana puree. Chill both purees for 2 hours in the refrigerator.

Serve in goblets or dessert dishes, half strawberry and half banana, garnished with sprigs of mint.

Variation

Cranberry Papaya Whip. For the strawberries, substitute 1 cup fresh cranberries covered with water and simmered until tender (5 to 8 minutes) before pureeing. For the bananas, substitute 2 ripe papayas, peeled and pureed. Increase the sugar to ½ cup.

Mango Fool

2 ripe mangoes
2 tablespoons lemon juice
1 cup heavy cream
1 tablespoon confectioner's sugar
4 lime slices

Yield: 4 servings

Peel the mangoes and cut them in large chunks. Combine the mangoes and the lemon juice in a blender or food processor and blend on medium speed until the fruit is pureed.

Beat the cream and confectioner's sugar to the stiff-peak stage. Fold the mango puree into the whipped cream and chill in the refrigerator for an hour or two.

Spoon into 4 chilled parfait glasses. Garnish each one with a slice of lime and serve.

Variations

Guava Whip. Substitute 2 or 3 ripe guavas for the mangoes.

Pear Whip. Substitute 2 or 3 ripe pears for the mangoes.

Pear Avocado Mousse

2 over-ripe pears, peeled and quartered
1 over-ripe avocado, peeled and quartered
2 tablespoons lemon juice
2 tablespoons grated orange rind
2 tablespoons rum
½ cup chopped peanuts, hazelnuts, or walnuts

Yield: 4 to 6 servings

In this dish, the mousse effect is achieved by whipping, rather than by using gelatin, eggs, or cream. It actually works better with over-ripe fruits than with just ripe ones.

Combine all the ingredients in a blender or food processor. Process for about 1 minute on high speed. Pour the mixture into a glass dessert dish and chill in the refrigerator for at least an hour. Serve it cold.

Variations

Plum Avocado Mousse. Substitute 3 or 4 over-ripe plums for the pears.

Apricot Banana Mousse. Substitute 3 or 4 fresh apricots for the pears. Substitute 2 over-ripe bananas for the avocado.

Tropical Fruit Macedoine

1 cup cubed fresh papaya
1 cup cubed fresh pineapple
1 cup cubed fresh mango
2 ripe bananas, sliced
¼ cup rum
¼ cup shredded coconut

Yield: 6 servings

There was a time when we (especially those of us in the northern latitudes) virtually had to cross continents to come face to face with some of these fruits. How lucky we are that most markets now carry them as standard fare.

Toss the fruit lightly in a bowl with the rum. Chill in the refrigerator for at least 2 hours. Spoon the fruit into chilled goblets and garnish with the coconut before serving.

Passion Fruit Cup

2 ripe passion fruits
1 tablespoon honey
2 tablespoons lime juice
1 banana
1 apple
1 cup seedless grapes

Yield: 2 to 3 servings

Because it flowers in an extraordinarily pictorial way, this tropical plant is named for the Passion of Christ. Until you develop a taste for its intensely sweet fruit, it may be best to sample it in conjunction with other fruits of blander flavor.

Cut the tops from the passion fruits and scoop out the flesh. Pick or sieve out the seeds. Mix the flesh with the honey and lime juice.

Peel and slice the banana. Peel, core, and slice the apple. Toss all the fruit together for an even distribution. Serve the fruit cup cold, in goblets or punch cups.

Note: For a different texture, leave the seeds in the pulp of the passion fruit. They are crunchy, tasty little morsels considered a great delicacy in some tropical lands.

Watermelon Bowl

1 medium-size watermelon
6 small apples
3 tangerines
10 canned lychees
6 fresh kumquats
1 cup raspberries

Yield: 6 to 8 servings

Of course you can do this with nearly any melon, filling it with any fruit. But here is a splendid and festive dish which concluded a Chinese banquet I once attended.

The Chinese often carve intricate designs or calligraphy on the sides of the melon shell, and sometimes the bowl is turned into a basket by leaving a handle of melon shell in the side that is carved away. But for most of us, notching the edge of the bowl is art enough.

Cut the watermelon in half, crosswise if you want a deep bowl, lengthwise if you prefer a longer, shallower one. (Save half the melon in the refrigerator for another day.) Scoop the pulp out of the melon, leaving a shell ¾ inch thick. Notch or scallop the top edge of the melon.

Discard the seeds and cube the watermelon pulp (if you have a melon baller, shape it into balls). Peel, core, and cut the apples into wedges. Peel, string, and section the tangerines. Drain the canned lychees. Wash the kumquats but leave them whole.

Toss these fruits, together with the raspberries, in a bowl to distribute them for color and texture contrasts. Pour them into the watermelon bowl, and chill the whole arrangement thoroughly before serving it at the end of your banquet.

Pineapple Pot

1 large ripe pineapple
1 cup fresh raspberries
1 cup red or purple grapes
½ cup watermelon balls
½ cup cantaloupe balls
½ cup honeydew or Casaba balls
½ cup fruit brandy

Yield: 4 to 5 servings

The prickly hard shell of the pineapple has to be good for something!

Slice across the pineapple 2 to 3 below the stem. Scoop out the flesh from the pineapple, leaving a ½-inch shell. Discard the core and chop the pulp into small pieces.

Combine the pineapple pulp with the rest of the fruit in a glass dish. Toss all the fruit with the liqueur, cover, and chill in the refrigerator for an hour or two.

At dessert time, pour the fruit and syrup into the hollowed-out pineapple and serve it, cold, from this unusual pot.

3
QUICK CUSTARDS, MOLDS, AND FOOLS

A brief period of stewing, or sometimes with no more than it takes to bring a cup of water to a boil, can transform all manner of fruit into splendid works of art. A little mixing, whipping, beating, whisking — accomplished by hand — will do wonders for your reputation as a dessert chef. And, of course, a blender or food processor will save you much labor with no compromise on quality.

Many of the desserts in the following pages combine fruits with eggs, cream, sour cream, or yogurt. An ancient and honorable tradition, the blending of fresh fruits and dairy products is more than the sum of its parts — both are enhanced by the union.

There are two opposite bits of advice to bear in mind concerning whipping cream and beating egg whites. When whipping cream, it's best to start with everything chilled, both ingredients and utensils. But this is not the case with egg whites; for better results, allow them to warm to room temperature before beating. And don't dismiss as an old wives' tale the notion that beating egg whites in a copper bowl produces more volume; it is a matter of verifiable fact. I was gifted some years ago with a large copper mixing bowl, and the meringues I've whipped up ever since have been markedly bigger and better!

Melon Cream

⬥△▽⬥△▽⬥△▽⬥△▽⬥△▽⬥△▽⬥△▽⬥△▽⬥△▽⬥△▽⬥△▽⬥△▽⬥△▽⬥△▽⬥△▽⬥△▽⬥△▽⬥

⅓ **cup sugar**
½ **cup water**
½ **cup orange juice**
1 ripe cantaloupe
1 tablespoon orange liqueur
½ **cup sour cream**
1 tablespoon grated orange rind
   (optional)

Yield: 6 to 8 servings

Although cantaloupe when perfectly ripe and sweet, served plain or with a little sherbet added, cannot be improved upon — here is a cool dessert that makes a lovely conclusion to a meal featuring poultry or fish.

For a subtle change of flavor (and color), substitute 1 juicy, ripe honeydew or Casaba for the cantaloupe.

Make a syrup by combining the sugar with the water and orange juice, bringing it to a boil, and then simmering for 5 minutes.

Peel and cube the cantaloupe; puree it in a blender or food processor.

Add the liqueur to the syrup; stir into the pureed cantaloupe. Stir in the sour cream.

Spoon the mixture into champagne glasses and chill in the refrigerator for at least an hour. Garnish with the grated rind just before serving.

Gooseberry Fool

1 pint fresh gooseberries
5 tablespoons sugar or to taste
1 cup heavy cream

Yield: 4 to 6 servings

Gooseberry Fool, which originated in England, may be the grandaddy of all desserts so called, and may be where the dish got its name (a goose is not only a bird, of course, but a name for a foolish person). But a more likely derivation is from the French word feuillet, *a fold or a layer (in cooking). Some dessert-creators I know make the outrageous claim that this dessert is called fool because it is so simple any child can make it with ease.*

In a saucepan, cover the gooseberries with water and simmer for 4 to 5 minutes, until they are tender. Drain and combine them in a blender or food processor with the sugar. Puree the fruit and sugar. Then put it through a fine strainer. Chill in the refrigerator for at least 1 hour.

Whip the cream to the soft-peak stage. Then fold it into the fruit puree, gently and carefully, so that it makes streaks and swirls. Serve the fool immediately in chilled goblets or dessert dishes.

Variations

Guava Fool. For the gooseberries, substitute 4 to 6 ripe guavas, blossom ends trimmed off, cut in 1-inch pieces.

Mango Fool. For the gooseberries, substitute 4 to 5 ripe mangoes, peeled and cut in chunks.

Peach Fool. For the gooseberries, substitute 4 to 6 ripe peaches, peeled and cut in chunks.

Nectarine Fool. For the gooseberries, substitute 4 to 6 ripe nectarines, cut in chunks.

Pineapple Fool. For the gooseberries, substitute 4 cups fresh pineapple chunks.

Chocolate Apricot Mousse

½ cup sugar
¼ cup white wine
2 tablespoons orange juice
6 fresh apricots, peeled and halved
2 cups heavy cream
1 teaspoon vanilla extract
1 cup shaved bittersweet chocolate

Yield: 5 to 6 servings

Chocolate harmonizes with and plays off any number of fruits in exciting ways. Try the flavor contrasts offered by these fruits.

Combine the sugar, wine, and orange juice. As soon as the sugar dissolves, add the apricots. Simmer this mixture over low heat for about 10 minutes, or until the fruit is softened.

Remove the apricots (reserving the liquid for Fruit Sauce, page 165) and puree in a blender or food processor. Chill the puree in the refrigerator.

Whip the cream with the vanilla until stiff. Fold the apricot puree into the whipped cream. Fold in the chocolate. Serve the mousse cold, in goblets or dessert dishes.

Variations

Chocolate Peach Mousse. Substitute 3 to 4 fresh peeled peaches, cut in half, for the apricots.

Chocolate Persimmon Mousse. Substitute 4 to 5 fresh persimmons, peeled and cut in chunks, for the apricots.

Chocolate Kiwi Mousse. Substitute 4 fresh kiwis, peeled and halved, for the apricots.

Grapefruit Snow

2 (¼-ounce) envelopes plain gelatin
1 cup grapefruit juice
1½ cups water
¼ cup sugar
½ cup sour cream or yogurt
2 egg whites
¼ cup shredded coconut
1 whole grapefruit, divided into sections

Yield: 5 to 6 servings

In the middle of a long, hot summer, this wintry dish makes a refreshing dessert.

Soften the gelatin in ½ cup of the grapefruit juice. Bring the water to a boil in a saucepan, add the gelatin and the remaining ½ cup grapefruit juice, and stir until it is completely dissolved. Stir in the sugar. Add the sour cream or yogurt.

Whip the egg whites until stiff, then fold them into the cooked gelatin mixture. Top with the coconut and chill in the refrigerator until the snow is set, from 2 to 4 hours. Just before it is completely firm, press the grapefruit sections into the top of the snow, in any pattern you fancy. Serve the dessert cold.

Applesauce Foam

2 or 3 small tart apples, peeled and diced
½ cup apple juice or sweet cider
1 cup water
1 (3-ounce) envelope any red gelatin

Yield: 5 or 6 servings

Simplicity itself is this fruit gelatin dessert.

Combine the apples and apple juice in a blender or food processor and blend at high speed until you have a smooth puree.

Bring the water to a boil, remove it from the heat, and stir in the gelatin until it dissolves. Pour the gelatin into a bowl and stir in the pureed applesauce.

Chill the mixture in the refrigerator until it is thickened a little, but not firm. Then whip until it is foamy and doubled in volume. Refrigerate until firm. Serve cold.

Variations

Pear Foam. Substitute 2 or 3 fresh pears, peeled and cut in chunks, for the apples.

Peach Foam. Substitute 2 or 3 fresh peaches, peeled and cut in chunks, for the apples.

Rhubarb Delight

4 cups water
2 cups sugar
¼ cup quick-cooking tapioca
6 cups 1-inch rhubarb pieces
2 (6-ounce) envelopes strawberry gelatin

Yield: 6 to 8 servings

Most people can't think of anything to do with rhubarb beyond sauce or pie. Try this cool and refreshing dessert the next time you have an embarrassment of rhubarb.

Put the water in a saucepan; add the sugar and tapioca. Over medium heat, stir this mixture until it thickens a little. Add the rhubarb and continue cooking for about 15 minutes.

Remove the saucepan from the heat; stir in the gelatin until it dissolves.

Pour the mixture into a glass dessert dish and chill in the refrigerator for 2 hours, or until it is set. Serve cold.

Papaya Mold

1 large ripe papaya
1 cup water
1 (¼-ounce) envelope plain gelatin
1 cup sherry
1 tablespoon crème de menthe
½ cup seedless grapes

Yield: 3 to 4 servings

A playful dessert with an interesting combination of colors and textures.

Slice the top off the papaya. Discard the seeds.

Heat the water to boiling, remove it from the heat, and dissolve the gelatin in it. Stir the sherry and crème de menthe into the gelatin and refrigerate for an hour or so, until it is partially firm. Stir in the grapes, distributing them evenly.

Pour or spoon the gelatin into the cavity of the papaya and replace the "cap." Chill the gelatin-filled papaya in the refrigerator for 3 to 4 hours. When the gelatin is firmly set, cut the fruit, crosswise, into ½-inch slices, and serve the slices cold.

Melon Mold

½ medium-size cantaloupe
¼ small-size watermelon
1½ cups water
1 (3-ounce) envelope pineapple or lemon
    gelatin
1 pint vanilla ice cream, softened

Yield: 6 to 8 servings

The incomparable flavor and texture of cantaloupe and watermelon are preserved in this dish (rather than altered, as they are in commercially frozen melon balls).

The sizes of the melon are arbitrary—what you want is enough cantaloupe and watermelon to provide 1 cup of each kind of melon balls.

Bring the water to a boil in a saucepan, remove it from the heat, and stir in the gelatin until it dissolves.

Chill the gelatin in the refrigerator until it is thickened a little, but not set. Stir in the ice cream. Fold in the melon balls.

Pour the mixture into a bowl or ring mold and chill it in the refrigerator for 3 to 4 hours, until it is set. Unmold onto a chilled platter and serve immediately.

Berry Tapioca

⅓ cup quick-cooking tapioca
2½ cups water
2 tablespoons lemon juice
¼ cup honey
2 cups fresh berries (blackberries,
   strawberries, raspberries, blueberries)
2 cups heavy cream

Yield: 4 to 6 servings

A fruity upgrading of tapioca pudding.

Put the tapioca in the top of a double boiler, add the water and cook over medium heat for 15 minutes.

Stir in the lemon juice and honey. Mash the berries a little and stir them into the pudding. Then let it cool.

Whip the cream until stiff, and fold it into the pudding. Serve the refreshing dessert, cool, in chilled goblets.

Variations

Peach Tapioca. Substitute 2 or 3 fresh peaches, peeled and cut in small chunks, for the berries.

Orange Tapioca. Substitute 2 or 3 fresh oranges, peeled, seeded, and cut in small chunks, for the berries.

Peach Charlotte

3 eggs
¾ cup sugar
1 teaspoon vanilla extract
⅓ cup milk
18 ladyfingers
3 ripe peaches
1 cup heavy cream
½ cup confectioner's sugar

Yield: 6 to 8 servings

A handsome, rich dessert, perfect for the finale to a light supper.

Separate the eggs. Beat the yolks lightly and stir in the sugar and vanilla.

Bring the milk to a boil; then reduce the heat to low. Add the egg-yolk mixture, a little at a time, stirring constantly, until it thickens. Let it cool.

Beat the egg whites to the soft-peak stage and fold them into the thickened, cooled custard.

Line the bottom and sides of a deep cake pan or baking dish with ladyfingers; pile the custard into the ladyfinger container, smoothing the top.

Peel and halve the peaches and lay them flat side down on top of the custard. Chill the dish in the refrigerator for 3 to 4 hours.

Just before serving, whip the cream and

confectioner's sugar until it is stiff. Top each portion with whipped cream as you serve it, cold.

Variations

Cherry Charlotte. Substitute 1½ cups of pitted, halved sweet ripe cherries for the peaches.

Pineapple Charlotte. Substitute 1½ cups of canned crushed pineapple, well-drained, for the peaches.

Berry Cream

1 pint fresh berries (blackberries,
blueberries, raspberries, mulberries)
2 cups sour cream
1 cup brown sugar

Yield: 5 to 6 servings

Don't be deceived by the modest list of ingredients: this is a luscious dessert, as elegant as it is simple.

Spread the berries in the bottom of a buttered 8-inch by 12-inch baking pan. Spoon the sour cream over the berries and sprinkle it with the brown sugar.

Place the pan 4 to 5 inches below a preheated broiler and broil for 5 to 8 minutes, just long enough for the sugar to bubble and melt. Serve the dessert warm.

4
FRUIT PUDDINGS AND SOUFFLES

Baking is the essential process in this chapter. All of the desserts in the next few pages spend some time in the oven, though a number of them are then cooled and served chilled. Some of these dishes are classic puddings enriched by fresh fruits, which add savor and succulence, and please the eye.

At all times and for all occasions do keep in mind the appearance of desserts, the way they strike the eye. Consider the following garnishes:

- Fresh mint sprigs—there's nothing quite like them, but what about other herbs, such as tarragon or thyme

- Curls of bittersweet chocolate, shaved off a square with a vegetable peeler

- Slices of fresh lemon, lime, orange, tangerine

- Candied citrus peels

- Black or golden raisins

- Chopped dates

- Whole, halved, chopped, or ground nuts

- Whole grapes, cherries, or berries

- Seeds: sunflower, sesame, guava, passion fruit, squash, pumpkin

- Rose, marigold, squash-flower petals

- Candied flowers

Or why not accent your fresh fruits with small fresh flower blossoms, such as violets, nasturtiums, yuccas, elderflowers? And if your dinner guests impulsively elect to eat them, don't despair. They are often eaten in salads—why not in desserts?

Berry Soufflé

1 tablespoon cornstarch
½ cup milk
3 tablespoons sugar
1 teaspoon vanilla extract
¼ cup heavy cream
1 quart fresh berries
6 egg whites

Yield: 6 to 8 servings

Stir the cornstarch into the milk until it forms a smooth mixture, then add the sugar. Cook over low heat until it thickens a little.

Let the mixture cool, then stir in the vanilla and cream. Mash the berries a little with a wooden spoon, and stir them into the creamy mixture.

Beat the egg whites until they are stiff; fold them into the berry mixture. Pour it into a buttered 1-quart soufflé dish.

Bake in a preheated 425° F. oven for 30 minutes. When it is finished, the soufflé will be puffed up and browned on top; serve it immediately.

Variation

Pear Soufflé. Substitute 4 to 5 peeled pears, cut into 1-inch chunks, for the berries.

Cherry Cheese Soufflé

1 pint sweet ripe cherries
3 cups ricotta cheese
1 teaspoon lemon juice
1 tablespoon grated orange rind
1 teaspoon vanilla extract
2 eggs, separated

Yield: 8 servings

In this easy dessert dish, the cheese and cherries provide interesting contrasts of flavor, texture, and color.

Pit and halve the cherries. Mix them with the cheese, lemon juice, orange rind, vanilla, and egg yolks, blending thoroughly. Beat the egg whites until stiff and fold them in. Spoon into a buttered 8-inch or 9-inch baking dish. Bake in a preheated 350° F. oven for 50 minutes, or until firm. Serve warm or cold.

Variations

Apple Cheese Soufflé. For the cherries, substitute 3 or 4 sweet apples, peeled and diced. Add 1 teaspoon cinnamon.

Nectarine Cheese Soufflé. For the cherries, substitute 3 or 4 fresh nectarines, cut in small chunks.

Fruited Flan

2 cups sugar
4 eggs
3 egg yolks
3 cups milk
1½ teaspoons vanilla extract
1 to 2 cups sliced or whole fruits
(Tangerine, orange, or grapefruit
sections; sliced apples, peaches,
nectarines, pears; whole strawberries,
raspberries, blueberries, blackberries)

Yield: 4 to 6 servings

Fruit and flan — a classic combination, found in many cuisines of the Western world.

Melt 1 cup of the sugar in a saucepan over medium heat. Stir the sugar constantly, until it becomes a golden-brown syrup. Pour this syrup into a lightly buttered flan mold.

Beat the eggs and extra yolks, the milk, and vanilla, and the remaining 1 cup sugar until they become a frothy mixture. Pour into the mold.

Place the mold in a pan of hot water; bake in a preheated 325° F. oven for 1½ hours.

Cool the flan and turn it out onto a chilled serving platter. On top of the flan, arrange your favorite fruit. Serve cold.

Double Strawberry Custard

Custard

1 cup sugar
½ cup sweet red wine
1 tablespoon lemon juice
1 quart fresh strawberries, crushed
8 eggs

Sauce

1 pint fresh strawberries
¼ cup sugar
3 tablespoons frais de bois or amaretto

Yield: 4 to 5 servings

In a saucepan, combine the sugar, wine, lemon juice, and 1 quart of strawberries. Boil the mixture for 5 minutes, then put it through a fine strainer.

Beat the eggs thoroughly, and put *them* through a fine strainer, adding them to the strawberry mixture. Pour into a buttered flan mold or deep baking dish. Cover and place the dish in a pan of hot water. Bake in a preheated 350° F. oven for 45 minutes, then cool the flan 3 to 4 hours, or until firmly set.

Prepare the sauce by blending the remaining 1 pint strawberries, the sugar, and liqueur to puree, then putting the puree through a fine strainer. Unmold the chilled flan onto a chilled platter and spoon the sauce over as you serve.

Orange Sponge

2 to 3 fresh oranges
3 tablespoons all-purpose flour
1 teaspoon grated lemon rind
2 eggs
2 tablespoons butter or margarine, melted
½ cup milk, scalded

Yield: 6 servings

Peel the oranges, seed them, and cut them into chunks, retaining the juice. Stir the flour and lemon rind into the orange juice.

Separate the eggs and add the yolks to the orange juice, stirring each in separately. Add the butter and milk.

Whip the egg whites until stiff. Fold them into the orange juice.

Put the orange chunks into the bottom of a buttered 8-inch or 9-inch round baking dish, and pour the custard over them. Place the baking dish in a pan of hot water, and bake in a preheated 350° F. oven for 30 minutes. Serve the sponge warm.

Variation

Pineapple Sponge. Substitute 2 cups diced fresh pineapple and 1 tablespoon pineapple juice for the oranges.

Apple Pecan Delight

4 to 6 apples
2 eggs
1 cup chopped pecans
1 teaspoon lemon juice
½ cup brown sugar
1 cup heavy cream

Yield: 4 to 6 servings

If you have a windfall of apples of a tart variety, here is a dessert that will make the best of it. Pecans are a lovely accent but, of course, other nuts will do fine, too.

Core and dice the apples into pieces no more that ½-inch thick, leaving the skins on. You should have 4 cups.

Separate the eggs; beat the yolks slightly. Combine the nuts, lemon juice, and sugar, and stir these ingredients into the egg yolks. Stir the apples into this mixture.

Beat the egg whites stiff, and fold them into the apple mixture. Spoon this batter into a buttered 8-inch or 9-inch baking dish.

Place the dish in a pan of hot water and bake in a preheated 350° F. oven for 40 to 50 minutes, until it is set and browned on top.

Serve the dessert warm, with heavy cream poured over at the last minute. (If this last touch adds too much in the way of cholesterol or calories, omit it, or substitute low-fat yogurt.)

Variation

Fresh Plum Delight. Substitute 4 to 6 fresh plums for the apples and pit, peel, and chop them. Increase the sugar to 1 cup.

Persimmon Pudding

2 eggs
2 to 2½ cups persimmon pulp
1 cup brown sugar
1 teaspoon cinnamon
1 teaspoon nutmeg
2 teaspoons vanilla extract
½ cup buttermilk
2 cups all-purpose flour
1 teaspoon baking soda
1 cup chopped nuts (pecans, walnuts, almonds, or a combination)

Yield: 6 servings

In a bowl, beat the eggs lightly; add the persimmon, sugar, and spices. Stir in the vanilla and buttermilk.

Sift together the flour and baking soda. Mix the dry and moist ingredients, stirring them just a little. Pour the mixture into a buttered 8-inch round baking dish. Sprinkle the nuts on top.

Bake the pudding in a preheated 350° F. oven for 45 minutes. Serve hot or cold.

Variations

Plum Pudding. Substitute 2 to 2½ cups fresh plum pulp for the persimmon pulp.

Mango Pudding. Substitute 2 to 2½ cups fresh mango pulp for the persimmon pulp.

Papaya Pudding. Substitute 2 to 2½ cups fresh papaya pulp for the persimmon pulp.

Berry Bread Pudding

2 cups water
1 quart berries (blueberries, blackberries, raspberries, or any sweet berry)
1 cup sugar
Butter
8 slices white bread
1 cup heavy cream

Yield: 4 to 6 servings

Of course you can tear up the bread if you want, but it's just as easy to do a bread pudding this way.

In a saucepan, bring the water to a boil, add the berries and sugar. Reduce the heat and simmer for 10 to 15 minutes, long enough to soften the berries and make a syrup.

Butter the bread on both sides. Place 2 slices on the bottom of a 5½-inch by 11-inch loaf pan. Spoon a quarter of the berry syrup over the bread. Then alternate layers of bread and syrup.

Bake in a preheated 350° F. oven for 20 minutes. Cool, then chill the dish in the refrigerator.

Whip the cream until stiff. Serve the pudding cold by cutting crosswise slices and adding a dollop of whipped cream to each serving.

Cherry Rice Pudding

1 cup cooked white rice
1 pint sweet dark cherries, halved
¼ cup golden raisins
¼ cup black raisins
2 eggs
¼ cup water
¼ cup honey
½ teaspoon nutmeg
1 teaspoon vanilla extract
1 (13-ounce) can evaporated milk

Yield: 5 to 6 servings

Combine the rice, half the cherries, and the raisins.

Beat the eggs lightly with the water. Mix the eggs, honey, nutmeg, vanilla, and evaporated milk, blending them into a smooth sauce. Pour this sauce over the cherry-rice mixture; then spoon the pudding into a buttered round 8-inch or 9-inch baking dish.

Bake in 350° F. oven for about 50 minutes, or until the custard is set. Serve the pudding warm or cool, garnishing each serving with the remaining cherries.

Variation

Berry Rice Pudding. Substitute 2 cups fresh raspberries, blueberries, or blackberries for the cherries.

Fruited Indian Pudding

1 quart milk
⅓ cup yellow cornmeal
¾ cup molasses
2 tart apples, peeled and diced
1 nectarine or 1 peach, peeled and diced
¼ cup butter
1 teaspoon ginger
1 cup raisins
1 cup milk (optional)

Yield: 6 to 8 servings

In my Massachusetts childhood, Indian Pudding was a favorite dessert among children; the fruited version is popular among Connecticut adults.

In the top of a double boiler, scald 1 quart milk. Add the cornmeal and continue cooking, stirring occasionally, for 15 minutes. Stir in the molasses and continue cooking for another 5 to 6 minutes.

Remove the cornmeal mixture from the heat and stir in the butter and ginger. Stir in the apples, nectarine, and raisins, distributing the fruit evenly throughout.

Spoon the pudding into a buttered round 8-inch or 9-inch baking dish; pour the remaining 1 cup milk on top (for a softer top).

Bake the pudding in a preheated 325° F. oven for 1½ hours. Serve warm.

Macaroon Peaches

6 ripe peaches
1 cup macaroon crumbs
2 tablespoons butter or margarine,
  melted
2 egg yolks, slightly beaten
1 tablespoon brown sugar

Yield: 6 servings

Here's a way to glorify fresh peaches and salvage some macaroons that have gone stale.

Plunge the peaches into boiling water for half a minute, then into cold water. Peel, halve, and pit the peaches. Scoop out a little flesh.

Stir together the scooped-out peach flesh, macaroon crumbs, melted butter, egg yolks, and sugar. Arrange the peach halves, round side down, in a buttered baking dish; top each with some of the macaroon mixture.

Bake in a preheated 350° F. oven for 30 minutes, basting the peaches once or twice with the syrup that gathers in the baking dish. Cool to room temperature.

Serve the dessert cool, two peach halves to each diner.

5
TARTS, PIES, CRUMBLES, AND COBBLERS

Tarts—fruit pies—are one of the jewels of creation. Lining a baking dish with pastry dough, then slicing up fruit, tossing it in sugar and spice, and slipping it into the oven for an hour seems a simple route to a sense-tingling, soul-satisfying dessert. And there are no mysteries to achieving a marvelously good crust, whether you put it under or over the fruit.

A hand-held pastry blender may help in combining shortening with flour; but I've always found "cutting in" accomplished just as expeditiously with two blunt table knives, one in each hand, making parallel cuts in opposite directions. For some doughs, hands are the best tools. In any case, use your bare hands to shape the dough into a ball; and chill the ball for at least a half hour in the refrigerator to facilitate rolling it out to the desired thickness and shape.

The phrase "easy as pie" does not immediately leap to mind when we consider the problem of keeping a bottom crust crisp and dry. Even a prebaked tart shell can lose its crunch in the further baking, as fruits soften and the luscious juices start flowing and bubbling. To avoid a soggy bottom crust, before adding the fruit filling, brush the dough with an egg white beaten until stiff, or spread a thin layer of fruit jelly or marmalade over the dough, or sprinkle over the dough a layer of closely packed toasted bread crumbs or cookie crumbs.

Now try a few of the confections that have been delighting my guests for decades and sustaining my family for generations.

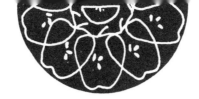

Foolproof Pastry

1 cup lard
½ cup water
3 cups all-purpose flour
1 teaspoon baking powder
1 teaspoon salt

Yield: Three 9-inch pie or tart shells

Break the lard into ½-inch pieces. Bring the water to a boil and pour it over the lard. With an electric mixer on low speed, blend the lard until it's smooth, then chill it in the refrigerator for at least 1 hour.

Meanwhile, sift together the flour, baking powder, and salt. Cut the chilled shortening into the flour until coarse crumbs form. Shape the dough into 3 equal-size balls; roll each out on a floured surface.

Fit the dough into pie plates or flan molds, crimp the edges, prick the bottoms and sides of the pastry with a fork. If you will use only one pie shell in the next day or two, put the other two, pie plates and all, in the freezer.

Bake in a preheated 425° F. oven for 15 minutes, or until the pastry is golden brown. Cool before filling.

Butter Pastry

1 cup butter
2 cups all-purpose flour
½ teaspoon salt
¼ to ½ cup ice water

Yield: Two 9-inch pie or tart shells

This is a richer pastry than the previous one. And it is made cold. All utensils and ingredients should be chilled before you start.

Cut the chilled butter into ½-inch pieces. Sift together the flour and salt. Put all these ingredients into a large bowl, sprinkle a tiny bit of the ice water over them, and work the pastry with your hands to mix in the water.

Keep adding drops of ice water as you blend, until you have a soft, glossy ball of dough. Divide the dough in half, form new balls, wrap them in waxed paper, and chill them in the refrigerator for at least an hour. Then roll them out on a floured board.

For tart shells, fit the dough into pie plates or flan molds, crimp the edges, prick the bottoms and sides with a fork.

Bake in a preheated 425° F. oven for 15 minutes, or until the pastry is golden brown. Cool before filling.

Variation

Half-and-Half Crust. Pastry made with butter may not be as flaky and tender as a shortening pastry. For a compromise, try substituting ½ cup margarine for ½ cup of the butter.

Graham Cracker Shell

1 tablespoon butter
1 cup graham cracker crumbs
1 teaspoon cinnamon
1 tablespoon sugar
1 egg

Yield: One 8-inch or 9-inch pie or tart shell

Melt the butter and cool it. In a mixing bowl, combine the graham cracker crumbs with the cinnamon and sugar, blending them well. Beat the egg lightly, add it to the melted butter and stir the moist ingredients into the dry.

Push the moistened crumbs into the bottom and sides of a pie plate. Bake for 10 to 12 minutes in a preheated 350° F. oven. Cool before filling.

Variation

Quick Light Graham Cracker Shell. Press 1 cup graham cracker crumbs into a pie plate; melt 1 tablespoon margarine and drizzle it over the crumbs. Then add the filling.

Nut Pastry Shell

½ **cup all-purpose flour**
½ **cup whole wheat flour**
½ **cup chopped nuts (walnuts, pecans, macadamias, almonds, cashews, or a combination)**
1 **teaspoon grated orange rind**
4 **tablespoons butter, chilled, broken into ½-inch pieces**
1 **tablespoon orange juice, chilled**

Yield: One 9-inch pie or tart shell

This is a good shell to use with bland fillings, but it also makes a fine underpinning for any number of fruit tarts.

Stir the two flours together, blending them well, then stir in the nuts and orange rind, distributing them well.

Cut the chilled butter into the flour mixture until coarse crumbs form. Then work the dough with your hands, adding the orange juice drop by drop, until you have a moist ball of dough. Roll it out on a floured surface.

Fit the dough into a pie plate or flan mold; prick the bottom and sides with a fork. Bake in a preheated 425° F. oven for 15 minutes, or until the pastry is golden brown. Cool before filling.

Guava Tart

6 fresh ripe guavas
¼ cup lime juice
1 tablespoon arrowroot
2 tablespoons water
1 baked 9-inch tart shell (pages 73 to 77)
1 cup heavy cream

Yield: 6 to 8 servings

Halve 3 of the juiciest guavas and, in an orange squeezer, squeeze out the juice. Strain the guava juice; then boil until the volume is reduced by a third. Reduce the heat to low and stir in the lime juice.

Dissolve the arrowroot in the water and add it to the guava-lime juice. Simmer this mixture, stirring constantly, until it forms a light syrup. Remove it from the heat and brush a thin coating over the surface of the baked crust.

Peel and halve the remaining 3 guavas and arrange them, flat side down, in the shell. Pour the remaining syrup over the fruit and let it cool to room temperature.

Whip the cream until it is stiff. Serve the tart cool and top each serving with a dollop of whipped cream.

Persimmon Tart

3 ripe persimmons
2 teaspoons baking soda
1 cup whole wheat or rye flour
½ teaspoon ginger
½ teaspoon nutmeg
½ cup raisins
½ cup chopped nuts
1 tablespoon butter or margarine, melted
1 tablespoon molasses
1 baked 9-inch tart shell (pages 73 to 77)

Yield: 6 to 8 servings

A perfect persimmon is such a beautiful artifact that it merits beholding for an hour or two before you put it into this delicious dessert.

Peel the persimmons, then cut up the pulp and mash it a little.

Combine the baking soda with the flour, ginger, and nutmeg and mix well. Stir in the raisins and chopped nuts.

Combine the butter and molasses and stir this mixture into the dry ingredients. Stir in the persimmon pulp until you have a homogeneous blend.

Spoon this filling into the tart shell, smooth the top, and bake in a preheated 350° F. oven for an hour. Serve the tart warm.

Berry Pear Tart

5 large ripe pears
1 cup orange juice
1 baked 9-inch tart shell (pages 73 to 77)
½ cup ripe blackberries, raspberries, or blueberries
⅓ cup pine nuts
¼ cup fruit brandy

Yield: 6 to 8 servings

An easy dessert to make; and its contrasting tones, textures, and flavors are a treat for the eyes and palate.

Peel and core the pears and cut them into ¼-inch wedges. Pour the orange juice over the pear wedges and let them marinate for 30 minutes. Then drain the wedges and overlap them in a circle around the edge of the pie shell.

Place the berries in the center of the shell; then drop the pine nuts on the fruit, distributing them all over. Sprinkle the brandy over the fruit.

Bake in a preheated 375° F. oven for 40 minutes, or until the pears are golden brown. Serve warm or cold.

Tart Apple Tart

4 to 5 tart cooking apples
5 tablespoons sugar
1 egg
½ cup heavy cream
2 tablespoons all-purpose flour
1 tablespoon cointreau or calvados
1 baked 9-inch tart shell (pages 73 to 77)
½ cup currant jelly

Yield: 6 to 8 servings

Peel and core the apples and cut them into ½-inch slices. Toss the apple slices in a bowl with 4 tablespoons of the sugar.

In an electric mixer, beat the egg and cream together at medium speed for 1 minute. Gradually add the remaining tablespoon of sugar, the flour, and liqueur.

Arrange the apples in overlapping circles in the tart shell and bake for 10 minutes in a preheated 350° F. oven. Then pour the custard mixture over the apples and bake for 15 minutes, or until the custard is puffed up and browned. Remove the tart from the oven and cool it on a rack.

Now put the currant jelly in a saucepan, bring it to a simmer, and cook, stirring, until it thickens to a syrup, about 15 minutes. While the tart is still warm, brush the syrup over the surface of the custard to glaze. Serve the tart at room temperature.

Berry Meringue Tart

4 egg whites
¼ teaspoon salt
½ teaspoon cream of tartar
1 cup sugar
1 quart fresh hulled strawberries, raspberries, blackberries, or blueberries
1 cup heavy cream
3 tablespoons kirsch

Yield: 6 to 8 servings

Contrary to the usual deployment, in this tart the meringue is underneath the fruit, in the place of a crust—in fact it is the crust.

Beat the egg whites, along with the salt and cream of tartar, until they are very stiff. Then beat in the sugar, a little at a time, until it is all absorbed and the meringue is glossy. Spoon the meringue into a buttered pie plate, pressing it very lightly into the sides and bottom.

Bake the meringue in a preheated 200° F. oven for 2 hours, then turn off the heat and leave the meringue shell in the oven until it cools completely, for another hour or so.

Pile the berries into the cooled meringue crust. Whip the cream with the kirsch until stiff peaks form. Spoon the whipped cream over the berries and serve the tart cold.

Variations

Peach Meringue Tart. Substitute 2 to 3 peaches, peeled and sliced, for the berries.

Nectarine Meringue Tart. Substitute 2 to 3 sliced nectarines for the berries.

Apricot Meringue Tart. Substitute 4 to 6 fresh apricots, quartered, for the berries.

Almond Plum Tart

⅔ **cup toasted almonds, minced**
½ **cup sugar**
5 tablespoons butter or margarine,
  softened
1 egg, lightly beaten
1 tablespoon flour
4 to 5 large ripe plums, halved
3 tablespoons apricot jam
2 tablespoons cointreau or cassis

Yield: 6 to 8 servings

Mix the almonds with the sugar. Blend the butter with the egg, then stir in the flour and almonds. Spread this mixture on the bottom of a 9-inch round baking dish. Arrange the plums, flat side down, on top of the almonds. Bake in a preheated 400° F. oven for about 40 minutes, or until the almond-egg mixture is set. Remove from the oven and cool on a rack.

Combine the jam and liqueur in a saucepan and simmer until the mixture thickens a little, 10 to 15 minutes. While the custard is still warm, spoon or brush the glaze over its surface. Serve at room temperature.

Variations

Almond Peach Tart. Substitute 4 to 5 ripe peeled peaches for the plums.

Black Currant Tart

2 cups dried black currants
1 cup water
1 unbaked 9-inch tart shell
   (pages 73 to 77)
¾ cup sugar
2 tablespoons quick-cooking tapioca
2 tablespoons sweet red wine
1 cup heavy cream

Yield: 6 to 8 servings

Simmer the currants in the water until they are softened, about 15 minutes; then drain them and put them in the tart shell. Sprinkle the sugar and tapioca over the berries; sprinkle with the wine.

Bake in a preheated 450° F. oven for 15 minutes; then reduce the heat to 350° F. and bake for another 30 minutes.

Whip the cream until it is stiff, and spoon whipped cream onto each wedge of the tart as you serve it, warm.

Prune Apricot Tart

16 large dried prunes
24 dried apricots
1 tablespoon minced lemon peel
1 tablespoon butter
1 baked 9-inch tart shell (pages 73 to 77)
5 tablespoons apricot jam or marmalade
1 cup pine nuts

Yield: 6 to 8 servings

This tasty tart made from "refreshed" dried fruits is even tastier when the fruits are soaked in wine rather than water.

Soak the prunes and apricots in enough cold water to cover them for 6 hours or overnight. Drain the fruit; pit the prunes and mince both the prunes and apricots.

Mix the lemon peel into the butter and set it aside.

With a fork, prick holes in the bottom of the tart shell, then spread the jam over the surface of the pastry. Spoon in the minced prunes and apricots. Dot the fruit with the lemon-butter. Sprinkle the pine nuts evenly over the top.

Bake in a preheated 350° F. oven for 45 minutes, or until the pine nuts are browned. Serve at room temperature.

Berry Cheese Tart

1 (8-ounce) package cream cheese,
  softened
1 cup cottage or farmer cheese
¼ cup honey
2 egg yolks
1 teaspoon cinnamon
1 baked 9-inch tart shell (pages 73 to 77)
2 cups fresh berries (blueberries,
  blackberries, or raspberries)

Yield: 6 to 8 servings

A beautiful dessert, perfect for following an entrée that has combined tomatoes, onions, and sweet or hot peppers.

In an electric mixer or food processor, beat the cream cheese, farmer cheese, and honey together until they are fluffy. Stir in the egg yolks and cinnamon. Spoon this mixture into the tart shell, smoothing the top. Distribute the berries evenly over the top.

Bake in a preheated 350° F. oven for 30 minutes. Cool the tart on a rack and serve it at room temperature. Or serve it chilled.

Nectarine Pie

¼ **cup all-purpose flour**
½ **cup sugar**
½ **teaspoon cinnamon**
5 to 6 **ripe nectarines, thinly sliced**
1 **teaspoon lemon juice**
2 **tablespoons butter or margarine**
1 **unbaked 9-inch pastry shell**
   (pages 73 to 77)

Yield: 6 to 8 servings

Combine the flour, sugar, and cinnamon and toss the fruit lightly in the mixture. Butter a 9-inch deep pie plate and spoon the fruit into it. Sprinkle the lemon juice over it. Dot the fruit with the butter.

Cover the fruit with the crust, crimping the edges well to seal it. Cut a few slices in the crust, or prick it here and there with a fork. Bake in a preheated 400° F. oven for 40 minutes. Serve it warm. Vanilla ice cream goes well with this pie.

Variations

Peach Pie. Substitute peeled sliced peaches for the nectarines.

Apple Pie. Substitute peeled sliced apples for the nectarines.

Sour Cherry Pie

6 cups pitted sour cherries
¼ cup quick-cooking tapioca
1 cup sugar
2 tablespoons orange juice
½ teaspoon vanilla extract
1 unbaked 9-inch pie crust
   (pages 73 to 77)
2 tablespoons butter or margarine

Yield: 6 to 8 servings

Sweet cherries present no problems to the dessert-maker. But their poor relations, sour cherries, should not be slighted. Here is a way to make glorious use of the succulent but piquant fruit.

Toss the cherries, tapioca, sugar, orange juice, and vanilla together to mix thoroughly. Spoon this mixture into a buttered 9-inch pie plate, distributing the cherries as evenly as possible.

Cover the fruit with the unbaked crust, crimp the edges, and cut slits in the crust or prick holes with a fork. Dot the crust with butter or margarine.

Bake in a preheated 450° F. oven for 10 minutes, then reduce the heat to 350° F. and bake for another 45 minutes, or until the crust is lightly browned. Serve either warm or cold.

Cherry Yogurt Tart

2 (8-ounce) packages cream cheese, softened
2 tablespoons frozen orange juice concentrate, unthawed
1 tablespoon grated orange peel
2 tablespoons sugar
1 cup plain yogurt
¼ cup water
1 (¼-ounce) envelope unflavored gelatin
1 baked 9-inch tart shell (pages 73 to 77)
1½ pints fresh cherries
2 tablespoons kirsch

Yield: 6 to 8 servings

There is something splendid about the melding of sweet, dark red cherries with the subtle tartness of yogurt, something very pleasing to both eye and palate. This handsome, festive dessert is very easy to make.

In a blender at low speed, or in a food processor, mix the cream cheese, orange juice and peel, 1 tablespoon of the sugar, and the yogurt; blend until the mixture is smooth.

Bring the water to a boil in a saucepan, remove it from the heat, and stir in the gelatin and remaining 1 tablespoon sugar until they dissolve completely. Stir the gelatin into the yogurt mixture, then spoon it into the tart shell.

Chill the tart in the refrigerator until it is set (2 to 3 hours).

Pit and halve the cherries. Top the tart with the cherries, sprinkle it with the kirsch, and serve cold.

Variations

Berry Yogurt Tart. Substitute 3 cups fresh strawberries or raspberries for the cherries and 2 tablespoons framboise for the kirsch.

Blueberry Yogurt Tart. Substitute 3 cups blueberries for the cherries and 2 tablespoons Armagnac for the kirsch.

Peach Yogurt Tart. Substitute 2 cups peeled sliced peaches for the cherries and 2 tablespoons Grand Marnier for the kirsch.

Mulberry Cobbler

¼ cup water
1 cup sugar
1 quart mulberries
½ recipe shortcake batter (page 116)
1 cup heavy cream

Yield: 6 to 8 servings

Some years ago, while visiting in Louisiana, I picked a quart of dark purplish-red mulberries. Resisting the temptation to turn them into liqueur (as my hosts periodically did), I made a cobbler of them.

Bring the water to a boil in a saucepan. Add the sugar, and when it is dissolved, reduce the heat and add the mulberries. Simmer for 10 minutes, stirring. Spoon the cooked berries into a buttered 9-inch round baking dish.

Prepare the batter according to the recipe directions. Drop by the teaspoon on top of the fruit. Bake in a preheated 375° F. oven for 15 minutes, or until the top is golden brown.

Whip the cream until it is stiff. Serve the cobbler warm, each serving topped with a dollop of whipped cream.

Variations

Gooseberry Cobbler. Substitute 1 quart fresh gooseberries for the mulberries. Increase the sugar to 2 cups.

Rhubarb Cobbler. Substitute 1 quart 1-inch slices fresh rhubarb for the mulberries. Increase the sugar to 2 cups.

Berry Cobbler

2 cups fresh berries (blackberries,
   raspberries, blueberries, boysenberries)
2 tablespoons lemon juice
1 cup sugar
1 tablespoon cornstarch
1 cup water
1 cup all-purpose flour
1 teaspoon baking powder
3 tablespoons butter or margarine
½ cup milk

Yield: 6 to 8 servings

Toss the berries with the lemon juice. Mix ½ cup of the sugar with the cornstarch, and sprinkle this mixture over the berries, stirring them around to coat them well. Spread the berries evenly in a buttered 8-inch square baking pan. Heat the water to boiling and pour it over the berries.

Sift the flour and baking powder together, and stir in the remaining ½ cup sugar. Cut the butter into the flour mixture and add the milk, a little at a time. Work it into a batter. Spread this batter over the top of the berries without any of it touching the edges of the pan.

Bake in a preheated 350° F. oven for 1 hour, or until the crust is very crisp. Serve the cobbler warm.

Peach Crisp

8 to 10 fresh ripe peaches, peeled and sliced
2 eggs, lightly beaten
½ cup brown sugar
1½ cups all-purpose flour
¾ cup butter or margarine
1 teaspoon cinnamon or nutmeg

Yield: 6 servings

Ring a change on good old classic Apple Crisp, the darling of so many country restaurants. If you wish to gild this particular lily, top it with whipped cream, sour cream, or yogurt. But it can stand deliciously well by itself.

Arrange the peach slices in a 9-inch or 10-inch round baking dish. Combine the eggs, sugar, and flour (don't mix them too zealously—leave some small lumps) and pour this mixture over the fruit.

Melt the butter and pour it over the crumb topping. Then sprinkle on the cinnamon or nutmeg. Bake in a preheated 425° F. oven for 1 hour. Serve it hot or cold.

Apple Crunch

1 cup uncooked rolled oats
½ cup sunflower seeds
¼ cup all-purpose flour
¼ cup brown sugar
½ teaspoon cinnamon
¼ teaspoon nutmeg
¾ cup butter or margarine
4 to 5 cooking apples, peeled and sliced
¼ cup chopped dates
1½ cups orange or grapefruit juice

Yield: 6 to 8 servings

Combine the oats, seeds, flour, sugar, cinnamon, and nutmeg, mixing well. Cut the butter into ½-inch pieces and cut into the dry ingredients until coarse crumbs are formed.

Arrange half the apple slices in a buttered 9-inch round baking dish, and scatter half the chopped dates over them. Sprinkle with half the oat-seed crumbs. Then layer on the rest of the apples, dates, and crumbs. Pour the juice over.

Bake the crunch in a preheated 375° F. oven for 45 minutes. Serve warm or cool.

Cranberry Crumble

1 cup Grape-nuts®, Cheerios®, or other crunchy dry cereal
½ cup all-purpose flour
1 cup brown sugar
½ cup butter or margarine, softened
2 cups cranberry sauce (with whole berries)
1 cup heavy cream

Yield: 6 servings

Betwixt bog and dinner table, the cranberry can undergo a marvelous transformation. In this tasty dish, the familiar, modest berry seems to enter another orbit.

Cream the dry cereal, flour, sugar, and butter together. Spread half this mixture over the bottom of an 8-inch square baking pan. Spoon the cranberry sauce over the layer of cereal mixture. Then cover the cranberry sauce with the other half of the cereal mixture.

Bake in a preheated 350° F. oven for 40 minutes, or until the top of the cobbler is firm. Cool on a rack.

Meanwhile, whip the cream until stiff.

When the cobbler has completely cooled, cut it into 6 squares and serve it at room temperature, each square topped with a dollop of whipped cream.

Rhubarb Crumble

2 cups fine bread crumbs
⅓ cup butter or margarine
3 cups 1-inch rhubarb slices
½ cup brown sugar
2 tablespoons orange juice
1 cup Grape-nuts® or other crunchy dry cereal
1 cup heavy cream

Yield: 4 to 6 servings

Spread the bread crumbs in the bottom of a 9-inch round baking dish. Melt the butter and pour it over the crumbs.

Cook the rhubarb with the sugar and orange juice over medium heat for about 10 minutes, until the rhubarb is softened. Spoon the fruit into the baking dish. Cover the rhubarb with a layer of dry cereal, then pour the cream over.

Cover and bake in a preheated 350° F. oven for 30 minutes, then uncover and bake for another 15 minutes. Serve this dessert either warm or cold.

Variation

Strawberry Rhubarb Crumble. Reduce the rhubarb to 1½ cups. When the rhubarb sauce when is cooled, stir in 1½ cups halved strawberries.

Apricot Nut Crumble

1 cup nuts (walnuts, pecans, hazelnuts,
   or a combination)
¼ cup whole wheat flour
¼ cup brown sugar
½ teaspoon ground coriander or allspice
¾ cup butter or margarine
8 to 10 ripe apricots, peeled and halved
¼ cup fruit brandy

Yield: 6 to 8 servings

Combine the nuts with the flour, sugar, and spices. Cut the butter into ½-inch pieces, then cut into the nut-flour mixture until large crumbs form. Place the apricots in a 9-inch round buttered baking dish and sprinkle the crumbs and brandy over the fruit.

Bake in a preheated 375° F. oven for 45 minutes. Serve warm or cool.

Variation

Plum Nut Crumble. Substitute 6 to 8 ripe red or purple plums for the apricots.

Green Apple Betty

½ cup butter or margarine
1 cup bread crumbs
4 to 6 cooking apples, peeled and sliced
2 cups brown sugar
2 teaspoons cinnamon
¼ cup lemon juice
¼ cup water

Yield: 8 servings

A delightful way to use some not-quite-ripe apples.

Melt the butter or margarine in the bottom of a 9-inch round baking dish. Add half the crumbs, then half the apple slices. Sprinkle them with 1 cup of the sugar and 1 teaspoon of the cinnamon. Then layer in the other half of the crumbs, apple slices, sugar, and cinnamon.

Combine the lemon juice and water and pour this over. Bake in a 350° F. oven for 50 minutes, or until the fruit is tender. Serve the betty warm or cool.

6
CAKES AND BARS

Strawberry shortcake is as American as, well, apple pie—a morning and evening star in the firmament of American classics; to omit it from a book of desserts is unthinkable. Nor would I consider any collection of fruit dishes complete without a dazzling, creamy cheesecake embellished with blueberries, peaches, pineapple, or whatever fancy or availability may dictate. But this is hardly the end of the marvelous ways that succulent fruits can bring a cake somewhere close to ambrosia.

One need not start with the perfect fruit caught at the very peak of ripeness for it to perform brilliantly in mixing bowl and oven. Over-ripe (nearly but not quite spoiled, to tell the hard truth) bananas make the best banana cake. Dried or canned figs, apricots, and prunes are especially delectable in tortes and bars. Hard pears and green apples, treated with due regard for their immaturity, are splendid bases for cakes and squares. Citrus juices contribute interesting flavorings.

Preheating your oven insures even cooking—a truth never to be overlooked. But the oven temperatures and baking times specified in this book should be read as approximate—a guide rather than a binding rule. No one unfamiliar with your oven and its quirks and peculiarities can tell you exactly how many degrees and minutes are necessary for best results; only you know that, from long trial and grievous error. You may find, too, that when you use glass ovenware, the oven temperature can be reduced a little.

A final tip: you can eliminate air bubbles and achieve a finer texture in a cake by sharply rapping your batter-filled pan once or twice on a hard surface, like a countertop, before you put your cake in the oven to bake.

Cheesecake I

1 (8-ounce) package cream cheese,
   softened
1 (14-ounce) can sweetened condensed
   milk
⅓ cup lemon juice
1 teaspoon vanilla extract
1 baked 9-inch graham cracker pie shell
   (page 76)
Fruit

Yield: 8 servings

*Top this cheesecake with fresh fruit for a
truly wonderful dessert.*

In a large bowl, beat the cream cheese with
an electric mixer at medium speed until it's
smooth. Add the sweetened condensed (*not*
evaporated) milk, a little at a time, while
continuing to beat. Stir in the lemon juice
and vanilla.

Pour the mixture into the crust. Chill it
in the refrigerator for 2 to 3 hours, or until
it is set.

Serve the cheesecake cold, each slice
topped with the fruit of your choice.

Cheesecake II

1 (¼-ounce) envelope unflavored gelatin
½ cup sugar
1 cup water
2 (8-ounce) packages cream cheese, softened
1 teaspoon vanilla extract
1 baked graham cracker pie shell (page 76)
1 pint fresh raspberries, blackberries, strawberries, or blueberries

Yield: 8 servings

Almost as easy to make as Cheesecake I, this cheesecake takes just as readily to a variety of fruit toppings.

In a large bowl, mix the gelatin and sugar. Bring 1 cup water to a boil, pour it over the gelatin and sugar. Stir until the gelatin is completely dissolved.

With an electric mixer or in a food processor, combine the gelatin solution with the cream cheese and vanilla until the mixture is creamy and smooth. Pour the mixture into the crust. Put the cake into the refrigerator and chill until it is firm, about 2 hours.

Spoon the berries, either whole or slightly crushed, over each wedge as you serve it, cold.

Variations

Peach Cheesecake. Peel and halve 3 to 4 fresh ripe peaches. Press them flat side down onto the top of the cheesecake and sprinkle them with lemon juice before you chill it. Omit the berries.

Cherry Cheesecake. Pit and halve 1 pint fresh sweet cherries, and spoon them onto the top of the cheesecake before you chill it. Omit the berries.

Pineapple Cheesecake. Drain 1 (6½-ounce) can pineapple chunks (reserving the syrup for Fruit Sauce, page 165), and spoon it over the top of the cheesecake before you chill it. Or use instead 2 cups crushed fresh pineapple, spooned over each wedge as you serve it. Omit the berries

Banana Cheesecake. Peel and slice 1 large or 2 small bananas, dip the slices in lemon juice, and arrange them on top of the cheesecake before you chill it. Omit the berries.

Plum Cake

1 cup butter or margarine
½ cup honey
2 teaspoons lemon juice
2 eggs, lightly beaten
1 cup all-purpose flour
1 teaspoon baking powder
½ teaspoon cinnamon
6 large purple plums, quartered
½ cup honey
½ teaspoon cinnamon

Yield: 4 to 5 servings

Cream the butter and ½ cup of the honey; then add the lemon juice and the eggs, stirring well to blend.

Sift the flour and baking powder together; stir in ½ teaspoon of the cinnamon. Combine the moist and dry ingredients, stirring them to a smooth batter. Spoon the batter into a buttered and floured 8-inch or 9-inch round cake pan, and smooth the top.

Arrange the plum quarters in circles, covering the batter. Drizzle the remaining ½ cup honey over the fruit; sprinkle it with the remaining ½ teaspoon cinnamon.

Bake the cake in a preheated 350° F. oven for 1 hour. Cool on a rack and serve at room temperature, cutting wedges as you would a pie.

Ginger Pear Cake

3 cups water
½ cup sugar
1 tablespoon lemon juice
3 large pears, not too ripe, peeled and
   halved
¼ cup all-purpose flour
1 teaspoon baking powder
1 teaspoon ground ginger
2 eggs
½ cup sugar
½ cup butter or margarine, melted
½ cup toasted almonds or peanuts

Yield: 8 servings

In a large saucepan, bring the water to a boil and add ½ cup of the sugar and the lemon juice. Stir until the sugar is dissolved, and reduce the heat. Add the pear halves and simmer for about 10 minutes. Drain the pears, reserving the liquid for Fruit Sauce (page 165).

Place the pears in a buttered 9-inch round cake pan, flat side down.

Sift the flour and· baking powder together and stir in the ground ginger.

Beat the eggs lightly, mix them with the remaining ½ cup sugar, then stir in the melted butter.

Combine the dry and moist ingredients and pour the batter over the pears. Top with the toasted nuts.

Bake in a preheated 350° F. oven for 45 minutes. Serve the cake warm or cool.

Simple Apple Cake

1 cup vegetable oil
1½ cups brown sugar
2 eggs, lightly beaten
2 cups all-purpose flour
1 teaspoon cinnamon
½ teaspoon baking soda
1 teaspoon vanilla extract
2 cups apple slices or cubes

Yield: 6 to 8 servings

Combine the oil and sugar in an electric mixer at a low speed until the mixture is creamy. Then stir in the eggs.

Sift together the flour, cinnamon, and baking soda and stir these dry ingredients into the wet ingredients. Stir the vanilla into the batter, and add the apple slices, distributing them throughout.

Butter and flour a 9-inch angel-food tube pan, and spoon the batter into it.

Bake the cake in a preheated 350° F. oven for 1¼ hours. Serve the cake warm or cold.

Variation

Simple Applesauce Cake. This cake can also be made with applesauce, if the sauce is not too runny. Substitute 1½ cups of applesauce for the apples. If the sauce is already sweetened, reduce the amount of sugar.

Blueberry Coffeecake

Cake

¾ cup sugar
¼ cup butter or margarine, softened
1 egg, lightly beaten
2 cups all-purpose flour
2 teaspoons baking powder
½ cup milk
2 cups fresh blueberries

Topping

½ cup sugar
⅓ cup all-purpose flour
½ teaspoon cinnamon
¼ cup butter or margarine, softened

Yield: 6 to 8 servings

A handful of that gallon of blueberries you picked will bring just the right touch to this easily made coffeecake.

Cream together the sugar and butter. Stir in the egg. Sift together the flour and baking powder. Add the dry ingredients to the moist, a little at a time, alternately with the milk. Fold the blueberries into the batter. (If you don't want them to "bleed" into the cake, roll them in flour first.)

To make the topping, cut the sugar, flour, cinnamon, and butter together, as you would for pastry, until it forms coarse crumbs.

Spoon the batter into a buttered, floured 8-inch or 9-inch square baking pan. Sprinkle the top with the crumb mixture.

Bake in a preheated 350° F. oven for 45 minutes. Serve warm or cool.

Peach Almond Torte

Torte

½ cup butter, softened
½ cup honey
½ cup all-purpose flour
1 teaspoon baking powder
2 eggs
½ teaspoon almond extract
½ cup ground almonds
4 ripe peaches, peeled and cut in ½-inch slices

Topping

1 tablespoon sugar
2 tablespoons all-purpose flour
1 tablespoon butter, cut into ½-inch bits

Yield: 6 to 8 servings

The flavor combination of almond and peach is wonderfully subtle.

Blend the butter and honey. Sift together the flour and baking powder. Beat the eggs lightly, stir in the almond extract. Stir all these ingredients together, adding the ground almonds and distributing them evenly throughout the batter.

Spoon the batter into a buttered 9-inch springform pan; smooth the top to an even surface. Arrange the peach slices on the batter in one overlapping layer.

Make a topping by combining the sugar and remaining 2 tablespoons flour and cutting in the chunks of butter until coarse crumbs form. Sprinkle the topping over the peach slices.

Bake in a preheated 350° F. oven for 1

hour. Cool the torte on a rack. Serve it at room temperature or cool.

Variations

Nectarine Almond Torte. Substitute nectarines for the peaches and don't bother to peel them.

Apple Pecan Torte. Substitute apples for the peaches. Substitute ground pecans for the ground almonds.

Fig Torte

½ cup ground almonds
¼ cup grated orange peel
¾ cup minced figs, fresh or dried
½ cup bread crumbs
½ teaspoon cinnamon
¼ teaspoon allspice
¼ teaspoon nutmeg
¼ teaspoon powdered clove
½ teaspoon baking powder
1 tablespoon amaretto or fruit brandy
   (more if using dried figs)
5 eggs, separated
¾ cup white sugar
Confectioner's sugar

Yield: 10 to 12 servings

Plum pudding may be a requirement for some people's winter holidays, but mine are never complete until I have made this splendid fig torte.

Mix the almonds, orange peel, figs, and bread crumbs. Mix the spices with the baking powder, and add them to the fig mixture. Add the liqueur, and mix all this with your fingers.

In an electric mixer, beat the egg yolks until they are foamy. Add the white sugar, a little at a time, and continue beating until the mixture thickens. Stir in the figs.

Beat the egg whites until stiff, and fold them carefully into the batter. Spoon the batter into a buttered, floured 9-inch springform pan.

Bake the torte in a preheated 325° F.

oven for 1 hour. Cool the torte upside down on a rack; remove the sides of the pan. Sprinkle the torte with confectioner's sugar before you serve it, cool.

Variation

Prune Torte. Substitute dried prunes for the figs.

Raspberry Brownies

2 eggs
1 cup sugar
½ cup sifted all-purpose flour
1 teaspoon vanilla extract
4 (1-ounce) squares unsweetened chocolate, melted
½ cup butter or margarine, melted
2 cups fresh raspberries
Kirsch or brandy (optional)

Yield: 16 brownies

In an electric mixer, beat the eggs on medium speed until they are light and frothy. Add the sugar, a little at a time, as you continue to beat. Stir in the flour and vanilla until the mixture is smooth; then stir in the chocolate and butter.

Butter a 9-inch square baking pan; then dust with cocoa or flour. Spread the batter in the pan.

Mash the raspberries to make a loose paste, and spread this topping over the batter.

Bake the brownies in a preheated 350° F. oven for 25 to 30 minutes. If the raspberry topping dries out too much, moisten it with a little kirsch or brandy when you take it out of the oven.

Cool the pan on a rack, then cut it into 16 brownies, each 2¼ inches square.

114

Pineapple Squares

2 cups all-purpose flour
2 teaspoons baking soda
2 cups brown sugar
1 (15-ounce) can crushed pineapple, with juice
2 eggs
1 teaspoon vanilla extract
1 cup chopped nuts (cashews, Brazil nuts, or ½ cup of each)

Yield: 24 squares

Because of its slightly "woody" texture and its high acidity, fresh pineapple tends to set some people's teeth on edge. If you belong to this group, canned pineapple in one of its forms is often on your marketing list. Canned crushed pineapple is the basis of this delicacy.

Sift together the flour and baking soda; stir in the sugar. Add the pineapple and juice, stirring in a little at a time.

Beat the eggs lightly and add them to the mixture, together with the vanilla. Add the chopped nuts last, distributing them evenly in the batter. Spoon the batter into a buttered, floured 9-inch by 13-inch baking pan.

Bake in a preheated 325° F. oven for 30 minutes. Cool the cake and cut it into 24 squares.

Strawberry Shortcake

2 eggs
2 cups sugar
1 cup all-purpose flour
1 teaspoon baking powder
½ cup milk
1 tablespoon butter or margarine, melted
1 pint strawberries
1 cup heavy cream

Yield: 6 servings

When you hear either of these words, you immediately think of the other, so inevitable is the association. Strawberry Shortcake is one of the most famous of desserts, and justly so.

With an electric mixer, beat the eggs until they are light and fluffy. Add 1 cup of the sugar, a little at a time, continuing to beat until the mixture is thickened.

Sift together the flour and baking powder; fold these dry ingredients into the egg mixture.

Heat the milk and butter to not-quite-boiling, and stir this into the flour-egg mixture. Spoon the batter into a buttered and floured 8-inch round cake pan.

Bake in a preheated 375° F. oven for 30 minutes. Cool the cake on a rack. When it is completely cooled, carefully slice it into 2 layers.

Halve the strawberries, slightly crush them with the remaining 1 cup sugar, and spoon half of the fruit on the bottom layer of shortcake.

Whip the cream until it is stiff. Top the fruit with half the whipped cream. Place the other layer of cake on the whipped cream and top it with the rest of the strawberries and whipped cream. Serve this classic, festive dessert at room temperature.

Variations

Berry Shortcake. Substitute a pint of raspberries, mulberries, or blueberries for the strawberries.

Peach Shortcake. For the strawberries, substitute 3 or 4 ripe peaches, peeled and sliced or cut in ½-inch chunks. Don't mash them.

Pineapple Shortcake. For the strawberries, substitute a (16-ounce) can of crushed pineapple, drained. (Save the syrup for Fruit Sauce, page 165.)

Banana Cake

1 cup brown sugar
1 cup butter or margarine
2 eggs, lightly beaten
1 tablespoon lemon juice
2 to 4 over-ripe bananas, mashed
¾ cup milk
2 cups all-purpose flour
1 tablespoon baking powder
½ cup chopped nuts
Cream cheese, softened (optional)

Yield: 8 to 10 servings

Here is a superb way to use up bananas that are over-ripe. For this cake, the riper the better.

Cream the sugar and butter; mix in the eggs. Stir in the lemon juice, bananas, and milk.

Sift together the flour and baking powder. Stir the dry ingredients into the moist. Add the nuts last, distributing them evenly throughout the batter. Spoon the batter into a buttered and floured 5½-inch by 11-inch loaf pan.

Bake in a preheated 350° F. oven for 30 minutes or so—until a crack appears on top of the cake. Serve it cool by cutting slices as if it were bread. (Some devotees like to spread their banana cake with cream cheese and eat it with a fork.)

7
FROSTY DELIGHTS

Frosty fruit dishes have been an important feature in most of the world's cuisines since time out of mind. Even in the days before refrigeration became a routine fact of life, ingenious cooks and homemakers fashioned raspberry sherbet on blocks of ice, whipped up lemon sorbet to be half-frozen in the ice box, and hand-cranked out batches of peach ice cream.

Ice cream, along with its near-relation sherbet, has been a favorite in America since its appearance here in the late 17th century. And—especially for an owner of an automatic ice-cream maker—it is an easy, foolproof dessert. But even if the freezing compartment in your refrigerator is the extent of your equipment, you needn't feel daunted by the exigencies of ice cream and sherbet making. The difference between light, fluffy tutti-frutti and an unappealing frozen lump is air. Yes, air. Automatic ice cream makers aerate by constant agitation during the freezing; the cook relying on a home freezer must whip, stir or whisk air into his or her preparation two or three times during the freezing. Frozen desserts from the supermarket include chemical emulsifiers and stabilizers; the home cook can substitute gelatin or eggs to stabilize ice cream, and a tablespoon or two of liqueur to prevent sherbet or sorbet from freezing to a block of ice. (Bear in mind, too, that a frozen dessert containing brandy or kirsch will melt faster at room temperature.)

Freezing means one thing to the person who possesses an electric ice cream maker: just follow the manufacturer's directions. It means something quite different to the dessert maker not so favored, who must follow these steps:

1. Pour or spoon your preparation into a freezer tray and leave it in the freezer for 2 to 3 hours, until partially frozen, with crystals forming around the edges of the tray.

2. Transfer the preparation to a bowl,

and stir or whisk it by hand for 3 or 4 minutes. Or, if breaking down whole pieces of fruit doesn't matter, whirl in a blender or food processor for 15 seconds.

3. Return the mixture to the freezer tray and replace it in the freezer for another 2 to 3 hours, or overnight. (This may be where you stop for some frozen dishes, but for ice cream, you will probably have to go on.)

4. Repeat step 2.

5. Repeat step 3.

6. If the consistency and texture doesn't please you when you spoon some out of the freezer tray, repeat steps 2 and 3 again.

It takes time and—lacking the machine that does the work for you—a bit of effort. But the results will be worth it. So take the time to become a frozen dessert chef on Thursday if you want gratifying compliments from family and friends on the weekend!

Scarlet Ambrosia

1 pint strawberries
1 pint raspberries
2 tablespoons apricot brandy

Yield: 4 servings

This sweet, rich, delicious finale is perfect for an otherwise bland or subtly flavored meal.

Combine the fruit and liqueur in a blender or food processor. Blend on medium speed until the mixture is nearly smooth.

Freeze in an ice-cream maker according to the manufacturer's directions or in a freezer according to the directions on pages 120 to 121.

Remove from the freezer 10 minutes before dessert time. Then spoon this brilliant froth into brandy snifters or parfait glasses and serve it at once.

Red Currant Crush

1 quart ripe red currants
¾ cup superfine sugar
1 teaspoon lemon juice

Yield: 4 to 6 servings

Note: Plain granulated sugar can be converted to superfine by a few spins of the blender or food processor.

Spread the currants in a single layer on a baking pan or cookie sheet; put the pan in the freezer, and leave it there for at least 3 hours.

Combine the frozen currants, the sugar, and lemon juice in a blender or food processor. Blend on low speed for 1 to 2 minutes, not so long that you do away with chunks of fruit. Serve in chilled goblets.

Variation

Berry Crush. Substitute 1 quart fresh blueberries, raspberries, or blackberries for the currants.

Passion Fruit Ice

1½ cups water
½ cup sugar
2 cups ripe cantaloupe or honeydew
   chunks
1 small ripe banana, sliced
4 ripe passion fruits
¼ cup lime juice

Yield: 4 to 6 servings

A cool, lush dessert for a warm summer evening.

Bring the water to a boil and dissolve the sugar in it. Cool this syrup, then chill it in the refrigerator.

Combine the melon and banana in a blender or food processor and puree.

Halve the passion fruits and scoop out all the pulp and seeds. Put the pulp through a sieve fine enough to extract the seeds. Press thoroughly to get all the juice possible. Add this juice to the cooled syrup, together with the lime juice.

Pour the syrup into a freezer tray and freeze for about an hour, or until slightly thickened. Then process the mixture in a blender at high speed or in a food processor for a few seconds—or until it is fluffy but not liquid.

Return the mixture to the freezer tray, cover it with foil, and freeze for 2 to 3 hours, or until it is almost firm. Beat it once more, quickly, put it into a sealed container, and freeze for 24 hours.

Soften the ice for 20 minutes at room temperature before serving.

Cranberry Frost

1 cup water
4 cups fresh cranberries
2 cups sugar
2 tablespoons orange juice
1 cup heavy cream
4 eggs
2 tablespoons Scotch or bourbon
½ cup chopped walnuts or chestnuts

Yield: 8 servings

At the age of 8, I danced across a school stage festooned in hundreds of cranberries strung on red string (performing the role of Cranberry Sauce in a Thanksgiving pageant). It was the end of my career in musical comedy, but not of the cranberries, which my frugal mother put to excellent use in this glorious dessert. I've been making it ever since, and can hardly imagine life without it.

Bring the water to a boil in a saucepan; add the cranberries and sugar. Reduce the heat to medium and simmer until the berries have softened, about 5 minutes; then remove them from the heat and cool.

Pour the cranberry mixture into a blender or food processor together with the orange juice and puree.

Whip the cream until stiff. Chill in the refrigerator.

With an electric mixer, beat the eggs until quite thick. Then, leaving the mixer on, add half of the puree to the eggs, a little at a time. Then add the liquor and continue beating for another 2 minutes. Stir in the nuts; fold in the whipped cream.

Freeze in an ice cream maker according to the manufacturer's directions or in a freezer according to the directions on pages 120 to 121.

Remove the dessert from the freezer 15 to 20 minutes before dessert time. Use the remaining puree for a sauce to spoon over each serving.

Melon Sorbet

½ **honeydew or 1 small cantaloupe melon**
1 **tablespoon sugar**
1 **teaspoon lemon juice**
1 **teaspoon fruit brandy**
Fresh mint leaves

Yield: 3 to 4 servings

Cut the melon pulp into large chunks and combine them with the sugar in a blender or food processor. Add the lemon juice and brandy and puree.

Freeze in an ice cream maker according to the manufacturer's directions or in a freezer according to the directions on pages 120 to 121.

Remove the sorbet from the freezer 10 to 15 minutes before serving. Garnish with mint leaves.

Variations

Pear Sorbet. Substitute 2 or 3 large ripe pears, peeled and cored, for the honeydew.

Mango Sorbet. Substitute 1 ripe mango for the honeydew.

Guava Pomegranate Sorbet

1 large ripe guava
1 cup water
⅔ cup sugar
2 tablespoons tequila
2 tablespoons grenadine
¼ cup lime juice
1 tablespoon minced lime peel

Yield: 4 to 5 servings

This is a potent pink sorbet, ideal for following a meal that is not highly spiced or flavored.

Peel, seed, and quarter the guava. Puree it in a blender or food processor. Bring the water to a boil in a saucepan. Stir in the guava puree and all the remaining ingredients. When the sugar is completely dissolved, remove the saucepan from the heat and cool.

Freeze the cooled mixture in an ice cream maker according to the manufacturer's directions or in the freezer according to the directions on pages 120 to 121.

Ten minutes before dessert time, remove the sorbet from the freezer. Serve in chilled goblets or parfait glasses.

Kiwi Sorbet

1 cup water
½ cup sugar
⅔ cup orange juice
4 to 5 kiwis
2 tablespoons lime juice

Yield: 6 to 8 servings

If you find that the novelty of handsome kiwi slices has worn off, you might want to use this most adaptable fruit in a different way.

Bring the water to a boil, stir in the sugar, add the orange juice, and simmer for 5 minutes. Cool the syrup and chill it in the refrigerator.

Meanwhile, halve the kiwis and scoop out the flesh. Combine with the lime juice in a blender or food processor and puree. Take care not to overprocess the kiwis, else you will shatter the seeds, which have a slightly bitter taste.

Stir together the puree and syrup, blending it thoroughly.

Freeze in an ice cream maker according to the manufacturer's directions or in the freezer according to the directions on pages 120 to 121. Serve it cold in champagne glasses.

Variations

Watermelon Sorbet. Substitute 2 cups diced watermelon pulp for the kiwis.

Guava Sorbet. Substitute 3 or 4 guavas for the kiwis.

Cherry Sorbet. Substitute 2 cups chopped sweet cherries for the kiwis.

Orange Sherbet

4 cups milk
2 cups water
1½ cups sugar
1 cup fresh orange chunks
1 cup orange juice
1 tablespoon grated orange peel
1 tablespoon lemon juice
1 tablespoon plain gelatin
½ cup warm water

Yield: 8 to 10 servings

In a saucepan, simmer the milk, 2 cups of water, and the sugar until the sugar dissolves. Raise the heat and boil the mixture for 5 minutes. Let cool to room temperature. Then stir in the orange chunks, juice, peel and the lemon juice.

Dissolve the gelatin in the remaining ½ cup warm water, and stir it into the orange mixture.

Freeze in an ice cream maker according to the manufacturer's directions or in the freezer according to the directions on pages 120 to 121.

Variation

Raspberry Sherbet. Stir 1 cup crushed raspberries into the sherbet mixture right after the dissolved gelatin.

Green Pear Sherbet

1 large ripe pear, peeled and quartered
1 cup water
1 (3-ounce) envelope lime gelatin
½ cup sugar
1 cup light corn syrup
1 (6-ounce) can frozen unsweetened
   lemonade concentrate
1 quart milk

Yield: 8 to 10 servings

There's something about the color green that makes us think cool. This lime-colored dish is perfect for clearing the palate and cooling the brow after a highly seasoned entrée.

Puree the pear in a blender or food processor. Bring the water to a boil and remove it from the heat. Stir in the gelatin, sugar, corn syrup, lemonade concentrate, milk, and pureed pear, blending well.

Freeze in an ice cream maker according to the manufacturer's directions or in your freezer according to the directions on pages 120 to 121.

Variation

Green Papaya Sherbet. For the pear, substitute 1 ripe papaya, peeled, seeded, and quartered.

133

Apple Blackberry Sherbet

½ cup water
2 cups apple chunks
¼ cup honey
¼ cup crushed blackberries
2 tablespoons orange juice
½ cup milk
2 cups fresh whole blackberries

Yield: 5 to 6 servings

This lovely sherbet makes a good dessert by itself, or with any fresh fruit topping. The apples and blackberries make a particularly handsome appearance and toothsome flavor combination.

Combine the water, apples, and honey in a saucepan and bring to a boil. Reduce the heat to low and add the crushed blackberries, orange juice, and milk. Cook this mixture for 10 minutes, then remove from the heat and cool.

Freeze in an ice cream maker according to the manufacturer's directions or finish in the freezer according to the directions on pages 120 to 121.

Remove the sherbet from the freezer 15 to 20 minutes before dessert time. Serve the slightly softened sherbet with fresh whole blackberries topping each dish.

Grapefruit Sherbet

1 large fresh grapefruit
1 (12-ounce) can frozen grape juice
   concentrate
1 cup white wine
½ cup plain yogurt
2 egg whites
2 tablespoons confectioner's sugar
Fresh mint leaves

Yield: 5 to 6 servings

A cool dessert to conclude a hot supper of chili, curry, or some other highly seasoned dish. This sherbet's color will remind you not so much of purple grapes as of lilacs.

Peel the grapefruit sections and halve them. Combine the grape juice concentrate, wine, and yogurt. Stir in the grapefruit. Put this mixture in the freezer and leave it until it is nearly but not completely frozen, from 2 to 3 hours.

Beat the egg whites until stiff, adding the sugar a teaspoon at a time. Fold the egg whites into the yogurt mixture. Return the sherbet to the freezer for 3 hours, or until it is completely frozen.

Leave the sherbet at room temperature for 15 to 20 minutes, then spoon it into parfait glasses, garnish with mint leaves, and serve.

Quince Sherbet

1 cup lemon juice
4 cups milk
4 ripe quinces, peeled and quartered
4 cups sugar
Mint sprigs

Yield: 4 to 6 servings

Combine ½ cup of the lemon juice with 2 cups of the milk. Using the finest side of a grater, grate all the quinces into the lemon milk. Drain the grated quince thoroughly through a fine strainer, and discard the pulp, saving the juice.

Add the sugar to the remaining 2 cups milk and bring it to a boil, stirring, until the sugar dissolves. Continue to boil for 5 more minutes.

Add the quince juice and the remaining ½ cup lemon juice, reduce the heat, and simmer for another 5 minutes. Cool.

Freeze in an ice cream maker according to the manufacturer's directions or in the freezer according to the directions on pages 120 to 121.

Remove the sherbet from the freezer 20 minutes before dessert time. Serve it cold, garnished with mint sprigs.

Frozen Berry Yogurt

2 cups plain yogurt
1¼ cups fresh berries (blueberries, strawberries, raspberries, or blackberries)
2 tablespoons orange juice
2 tablespoons honey

Yield: 4 to 6 servings

There's no reason to buy frozen fruit yogurt when it's so easy and economical to create your own flavors and combinations.

Stir together the yogurt, 1 cup of the berries, the orange juice, and honey, crushing the berries slightly.

Freeze in an ice cream maker according to the manufacturer's directions or in a freezer according to the directions on pages 120 to 121.

Remove the dessert from the freezer 20 minutes before you want to serve. Sprinkle a few of the remaining ¼ cup berries over each serving.

Variations

Frozen Peach Yogurt. Substitute 1¼ cups peeled, thinly sliced peaches for the berries. Use 1 cup for freezing, ¼ cup for topping.

Berry Ice Cream

4 eggs
1½ cups sugar
1 quart light cream
1 tablespoon plain gelatin
½ cup warm water
1 (12-ounce) can evaporated milk
1 teaspoon vanilla extract
1 pint berries (strawberries, blueberries, raspberries, blackberries), crushed

Yield: 8 to 10 servings

A basic ice cream recipe, adaptable to many fresh fruits.

Beat the eggs and stir in the sugar.

Heat the cream in a saucepan over medium heat to not quite boiling. Stir the egg-sugar mixture into the cream, a little at a time; continue cooking and stirring until a thick custard forms.

Dissolve the gelatin in the warm water. Remove the custard from the heat and stir in the gelatin. Cool completely, then chill in the refrigerator for 1 hour.

Combine the evaporated milk, vanilla, and berries; stir this mixture into the chilled custard.

Freeze in an ice cream maker according to the manufacturer's directions or in the freezer according to the directions on pages 120 to 121.

Variations

Peach Ice Cream. Substitute 2 cups crushed peaches for the berries and 1 teaspoon almond extract for the vanilla.

Avocado Ice Cream. Substitute a ripe avocado, pureed, for the berries.

Tropical Fruit Ice Cream. Substitute the flesh of 1 guava, 1 mango, and 1 passion fruit, pureed, for the berries.

Strawberry Pistachio Melba

2 cups strawberry jelly
1 cup light corn syrup
¼ cup cointreau
2 cups fresh strawberries, halved
1 quart pistachio ice cream

Yield: 6 to 8 servings

A suprising and delightful flavor contrast.

Combine the strawberry jelly and corn syrup in a saucepan. Stir this mixture over medium heat until the jelly melts. Cool and stir in the cointreau and the strawberries. Chill the fruit and syrup in the refrigerator.

At dessert time, spoon the ice cream into goblets or dessert dishes, and spoon the strawberry syrup over each serving.

Variations

Raspberry Walnut Melba. Substitute 2 cups raspberry jelly for the strawberry, 2 cups fresh raspberries for the strawberries, and 1 quart maple-walnut ice cream for the pistachio.

Blackberry Pecan Melba. Substitute 2 cups grape jelly for the strawberry, 2 cups fresh blackberries for the strawberries, and 1 quart butter pecan ice cream for the pistachio.

Apple Chocolate Melba. Substitute 2 cups apple jelly for the strawberry, 2 cups diced apples for the strawberries, and 1 quart chocolate-chip ice cream for the pistachio.

Chocolate Tangerine Freeze

Chocolate-covered graham crackers
1 pint heavy cream
1 cup shaved bittersweet chocolate
1 tablespoon orange juice
2 tangerines

Yield: 6 to 8 servings

This was my mother's answer to the challenge of making ice cream without an automatic freezer. It's surprisingly good.

Line a freezer tray, bottom and sides, with the graham crackers. Trim the crackers, if necessary, so that they are even with the edge of the tray.

Whip the cream until stiff. Fold in the chocolate shavings and orange juice. Spoon the mixture into the graham cracker form, smoothing the top.

Peel and section the tangerines. Press the sections lightly into the surface of the whipped cream.

Freeze the dessert for 3 or 4 hours, or until the cream is firm. Thaw it until you can cut slices across the width of the freezer tray, and serve it on chilled dessert plates.

Variations

Chocolate Orange Freeze. Substitute 1 large orange for the tangerines.

Chocolate Raspberry Freeze. Substitute 1 cup of whole fresh raspberries for the tangerines.

Chocolate Cherry Freeze. Substitute 1 cup of fresh sweet cherries, halved, for the tangerines.

Raspberry Bombe

3 pints Raspberry Sherbet (page 132)
¾ cup water
¾ cup sugar
4 egg yolks
1¼ cups heavy cream
1 tablespoon grated orange peel
¼ cup kirsch
3 cups fresh raspberries

Yield: 10 to 12 servings

An almost criminally rich dessert. Serve it after a low-key supper, perhaps of rice and vegetables.

Press the raspberry sherbet into the bottom and sides of a 2-quart mold. Freeze this shell until the sherbet is hard, at least 1 hour.

In a saucepan, bring the water to a boil, add the sugar, and boil until it thickens slightly.

With an electric mixer, beat the egg yolks until they are light and fluffy, then add the sugar syrup in a slow, steady stream. Beat this mixture for about 15 minutes, until it has cooled to room temperature. Cover it and chill in the refrigerator.

Whip the cream to the soft-peak stage and fold in the orange peel and liqueur. Then fold in the chilled egg mixture.

Spoon this mixture into the sherbet-lined mold and freeze it, covered, for 6 hours or overnight. Unmold the bombe onto a chilled platter and serve it at once, with raspberries spooned over each serving.

Variation

Strawberry Bombe. Substitute 3 pints strawberry sherbet for the raspberry sherbet, and 3 cups halved strawberries for the raspberries.

Watermelon Froth

2 cups pink watermelon flesh, cut in chunks
1 cup plain yogurt
¼ cup Raspberry Sherbet (page 132)
1 tablespoon shaved ice

Yield: 2 servings

Here is a gorgeous bubbly pink drink. And why not occasionally serve a cool, frosty dessert that you can drink?

Combine everything in a blender and run it on medium speed for about 30 seconds. Serve immediately.

Variations

Cantaloupe Froth. Substitute cantaloupe for the watermelon. For the raspberry sherbet, substitute orange.

Peach Froth. For the watermelon, substitute fresh sliced peaches. For the raspberry sherbet, substitute orange or peach.

Frozen Oranges

4 small seedless oranges
Orange or lemon sherbet
Curaçao or amaretto

Yield: 4 servings

This dessert features the lovely orange in a piquant new form, one that never fails to please as it refreshes.

Put the oranges, whole and unpeeled, in the freezer and leave them for 6 hours or overnight. Or for a couple of weeks.

About 30 minutes before you serve dessert, remove the oranges and let them thaw a little at room temperature.

At dessert time, slice the tops off the oranges. Spoon a layer of sherbet into 4 dessert dishes, and position the oranges cut side up in the sherbet. Carefully spoon a teaspoon or so of liqueur into each orange.

Serve the oranges immediately, along with small sharp spoons, and let your guests eat this frosty treat right out of its natural habitat.

Rainbow Cream

16 stale macaroons or amaretti
2 cups heavy cream
1 teaspoon vanilla extract
2 tablespoons sugar
1 pint Raspberry Sherbet (page 132)
1 pint Green Pear Sherbet (page 133)
1 pint Orange Sherbet (page 132)
2 cups fresh blackberries, blueberries, or
    raspberries

Yield: 10 to 12 servings

Break the macaroons into large crumbs. Whip the cream until stiff, then fold into it the vanilla, sugar, and macaroon crumbs. Spoon half of this mixture into the bottom of a freezer tray.

Spoon over the whipped cream a layer of each of the sherbets. Spread the remaining whipped cream mixture on top, and put the tray in the freezer. Leave it there for 3 to 4 hours, or until it is very firm.

Twenty minutes before dessert time, remove the tray from the freezer and place it upside down on a serving platter. If you can get the block of cream out intact, fine —serve it by slicing it carefully. If you can't extract it whole from the freezer tray, then cut slices *in* the tray, and serve with berries sprinkled over each slice.

8
MISCELLANY AND EXOTICA

In a collection of recipes as highly selective as this one, much is of necessity excluded. The possibilities for fruit desserts are endless, as you will discover when you begin to depart from received wisdom and strike out in new directions. What follows is a group of miscellany—dishes that did not readily fit into some other category, several of which are my personal favorites. And some exotic desserts, no less marvelous for being relatively unfamiliar. Some you will have heard of but not had the chance to sample; one or two you may have tasted once and long wished to taste again; and some you may never have heard of. All the better if the last is true, for here is a chance to enlarge your vision of the great world. Watch your family, friends, guests as they try the unfamiliar dessert, registering pleasure at the comeliness of what they see, and bafflement as to its precise nature.

Several of these dishes, for example, the American Indian specialties, in addition to providing an excellent dessert to conclude a meal or enhance an afternoon or evening party, will inevitably serve as conversation pieces. But principally they are here because they are not difficult to make, they taste good, and once you have tried them, you will find yourself adding them to your standard repertory.

Vanilla Pears

3 cups water
1 cup sugar
1½ tablespoons vanilla extract
4 large, firm, fresh pears, peeled and
  halved
½ cup fresh raspberries

Yield: 8 servings

One of my personal favorites, this is a very tasty way to treat pears.

Bring the water to a boil in a saucepan, then stir in the sugar until it dissolves; add the vanilla. Reduce the heat, add the pear halves and simmer them in the syrup for 15 minutes. Let the pears cool in the syrup for 30 minutes.

Remove the fruit from the syrup and transfer to a serving platter or bowl. Boil the syrup until it thickens a bit, and pour it over the fruit.

Chill the dish in the refrigerator for an hour or so. Serve 1 pear half to each diner, spooning some syrup and a few raspberries over each serving at the last moment.

Mint Pears

4 large ripe pears
2 cups water
½ cup sugar
¼ cup fresh mint leaves
Lemon sherbet or lemon ice cream
¼ cup crème de menthe
Mint sprigs

Yield: 4 servings

Pears combine well with many different flavors—especially mint.

Don't peel them, but, starting at the thick end, core the pears.

Bring the water to a boil in a saucepan; stir in the sugar. Reduce the heat and simmer for 8 minutes. Add the pears and the mint leaves and simmer for another 5 minutes, or until the pears are just a little tender. Remove the saucepan from the heat and let the pears cool in the syrup.

Chill the pears and syrup in the refrigerator for at least 1 hour.

At dessert time, spoon a little lemon sherbet into each dessert dish and set a pear in each one. Pour a little crème de menthe over each pear and garnish it with a sprig of mint. Serve at once.

Gooseberry Sticks

1 quart fresh gooseberries
2 cups water
2 cups sugar
1 tablespoon cinnamon
Confectioner's sugar

Yield: About 12 servings

From the Caribbean, this is an amusing way to render these tart berries into a confection to please any sweet tooth.

Stem the gooseberries, prick them with a fork, cover them with water, and soak for 6 hours or overnight. Drain them.

Bring the water to boil in a saucepan, stir in the sugar, and cook over medium heat until a thick syrup forms. Add the gooseberries and the cinnamon, reduce the heat, and simmer for 15 minutes.

Drain the berries (reserving the syrup for Fruit Sauce, page 165), and let them cool. Skewer the berries, about a dozen berries to the stick. Roll the sticks in confectioner's sugar, and serve them to a dozen bewitched diners.

Hot Candied Apples

3 to 4 crisp, tart apples
1 cup cornstarch
¼ cup water
5 cups vegetable oil
3 tablespoons peanut or sesame oil
¼ cup sugar

Yield: 4 to 5 servings

This is not the candy-coated apple on a stick that you prized as a child attending a state fair, carnival, or seashore resort, but a marvelous confection just as much fun as apple on a stick—and one of the most popular Chinese desserts.

Peel and core the apples and cut them in wedges.

Dissolve ½ cup of the cornstarch in the water. Roll the apple wedges in the remaining ½ cup cornstarch, then add them to the cornstarch paste, stirring them around to get them completely coated. Transfer the apples to a buttered, warmed platter or baking dish.

Heat the vegetable oil in a large wok or deep pan. When the oil is hot (about 365° F.), drop in the apple wedges, one at a time. When they are crackling hot and crisp, scoop them out with a strainer or slotted spoon. Drain them thoroughly.

Pour the sesame or peanut oil into the wok and heat it over medium heat. Add the sugar and stir, slowly at first, then quickly, until the mixture turns golden and bubbles. Reduce the heat, and when the bubbling stops, add the apples all at once. Toss the apples in the syrup repeatedly, so that each piece is thoroughly coated with the syrup. Serve the candied apples on a warm buttered platter.

Now comes the fun. Provide your diners with little bowls of ice water and forks (or if they can handle them, chopsticks). They dip their forks into the ice water, pick up a piece of the hot, sticky fruit, then dip the apple into the ice water, holding it under for 5 to 10 seconds. This will harden the sugar coating to the consistency of peanut brittle, and simultaneously cool the fruit enough so that it can be eaten without danger—and with delectation.

Imperial Applesauce

¼ cup raisins
¼ teaspoon saffron threads
2 tablespoons rose water
5 medium-size apples, the sweeter the better
1 teaspoon lemon juice
½ cup butter or margarine
½ cup half-and-half or light cream
¼ cup slivered almonds

Yield: 4 servings

If you don't have any saffron or rose water handy, substitute orange juice and you'll still have an apple dessert fit for a king, a queen, or a raj.

Crumble the saffron and add it to the rose water. Cover the apples with cold water and the lemon juice, and leave them for 5 minutes.

Heat the butter until foaming and remove it from the heat. Drain the apples and grate them into the butter. Cook over low heat, stirring, until all the liquid is gone.

Drain the raisins and add them, with the saffron-rose water, to the apples. Add the half-and-half and almonds and continue to cook until the mixture is quite thick.

Serve the dessert hot or cold.

Catawba Peach Soup

1½ cups fresh corn kernels
  (about 3 ears)
1 cup hot water
2 tablespoons sunflower seeds
1 teaspoon minced mint leaves
8 ripe peaches, peeled and diced
2 tablespoons pure maple syrup
1 teaspoon ground ginger

Yield: 8 to 10 servings

Here is dessert you can drink. It is a very special sweet soup, adapted from a recipe developed by Barrie Kavasch, ethnobotanist, authority on Native American foods and cookery, and friend. Barrie's recipe was based on a dish popular among the Catawba Indians of South Carolina.

Combine the corn kernels and hot water in a blender or food processor and puree them to a smooth corn milk, in 20 to 30 seconds. Add the sunflower seeds and mint leaves and puree for another 20 seconds.

Combine this puree with the diced peaches, maple syrup, and ginger in a large pot, and simmer, stirring occasionally, for about 30 minutes.

Serve this soup warm or cool, sprinkled with additional sunflower seeds and mint leaves or your favorite garnish.

Muckleshoot Raspberry Pudding

2 cups water
1 cup honey
2 quarts fresh raspberries
½ cup fresh red or black currants

Yield: 10 to 12 servings

Courtesy, again, of Barrie Kavasch, here is another native American dessert. This luscious, easy-to-make pudding comes from the Muckleshoot Indians, who live on a small reservation in Washington just south of Seattle, where there is a great abundance of wild raspberries.

In a saucepan, bring the water to a boil, add the honey, and boil for 10 minutes. Reduce the heat, add the raspberries and currants, and simmer for 10 minutes more. Cool the pudding and serve it in goblets or dessert dishes.

Baked Banana

1 not-quite-ripe banana
1 teaspoon honey
1 teaspoon shredded coconut, or
   1 teaspoon shaved chocolate, or both

Yield: 1 serving

If you have brought home from the market some green bananas and you can't wait for them to mature—here's a tasty fate for one of them.

Peel, destring, and slice the banana in half lengthwise. Place it flat side up in a buttered baking dish. Cover both halves with honey and sprinkle them with coconut and/or chocolate. Bake the banana in a 350° F. oven for 12 to 15 minutes, until the coconut is browned. Eat it with a spoon or fork.

Fried Banana Roll

1½ cups all-purpose flour
2 tablespoons sugar
6 tablespoons butter, softened
1 tablespoon cold water (more as needed)
4 small ripe bananas, peeled
Vegetable oil
Cinnamon

Yield: 4 servings

For this African specialty, use bananas that are ripe but not over-ripe, and small enough to be handled without falling apart.

Combine the flour and sugar in a bowl. Cut the butter into the flour mixture with a pastry blender or two knives. Add a tablespoon or so of cold water, a little at a time, until you can form a firm ball of dough. Wrap the dough in waxed paper and chill it in the refrigerator for about 30 minutes.

Divide the chilled dough into 4 parts and roll them out into ovals on a floured surface. Lay a banana on each oval and roll it up in the pastry, sealing the edges and ends with your fingers.

Pour vegetable oil into a wok or frying

pan to depth of 1 inch. Heat the oil to about 365° F. Add the rolls, and fry for 3 or 4 minutes on each side, until the pastry is crisp and golden. Drain the banana rolls. Serve warm, sprinkled with cinnamon.

Fritters 'n Fruit

4 cups large-curd cottage cheese
4 egg yolks
⅔ cup all-purpose flour
2 tablespoons sugar
½ pound butter, melted
1 cup sour cream
Fruit

Yield: 4 to 6 servings

The sweet cheese fritter with sour cream is a typical Russian dessert.

Put the cottage cheese in a colander, cover the cheese with a clean cloth or kitchen towel, then weight it with a brick or something equally heavy.

After the cheese has drained for 3 hours, rub it with a wooden spoon through a fine sieve. Stir the egg yolks into the dry cheese, and then the flour and sugar, a little at a time.

Shape this dough into 4 balls, then roll each ball by hand into a 1-inch cylinder. Wrap each cylinders separately in waxed paper; then chill in the refrigerator for 30 minutes.

When you are ready to fry, put half the butter in a saucepan over medium heat.

Meanwhile, cut the cheese cylinders into circles. When the butter is bubbling, fry half the circles, turning each one once, until they are nicely browned.

Now repeat with the remaining butter and the remaining fritters. Serve warm, with a dollop of sour cream and sprinkling of sliced or halved berries, cherries, peaches, nectarines, bananas, or the fruit of your choice on each serving.

Apricot Cheese Pizza

1 sheet frozen puff pastry
1 (15-ounce) container ricotta cheese
1 (3-ounce) package cream cheese, softened
½ cup confectioner's sugar
1 teaspoon grated lemon peel
8 to 10 fresh apricots, halved
¼ cup chopped nuts (pecans, walnuts, cashews, or pine nuts)

Yield: 8 to 10 servings

A really stunning dessert pizza, easily made with the help of some conveniences: frozen puff pastry and canned apricots, if desired.

Thaw the pastry on an ungreased cookie sheet. Bake it a preheated 450° F. oven for 10 minutes, or until it is golden and puffed up. Cool the pastry on a rack.

With an electric mixer, beat the ricotta, cream cheese, sugar, and lemon peel to a creamy smooth mixture.

Put the cooled pastry on a serving platter. Spread the cheese mixture over the pastry, leaving a ½-inch border. Arrange the apricots, flat side down, on the cheese. Sprinkle the pizza with nuts and serve it cold.

Fruit Sauce

2 cups poaching liquid
2 cups sweet or dry red wine
½ teaspoon cinnamon
½ teaspoon nutmeg
½ teaspoon ground cloves
2 seedless oranges, peeled, cut in small
   chunks

Yield: About 1 quart

Here is the Fruit Sauce you have been reading about all through earlier chapters. Any time you poach a fruit, save the liquid and use it as the basis of a sauce that you can use to top all manner of desserts: puddings, molds, cakes, ice creams, sorbets—or even plain, uncooked fresh fruits.

This is a basic recipe, subject to an infinity of variations, according to your taste and the fruits you have poached or stewed.

Combine all these ingredients in a saucepan and simmer for 15 minutes. If you want a smoother sauce, strain out the orange pulp.

Store this sauce in the refrigerator, where it will keep for about 2 weeks. Or freeze it and keep it no more that 2 months.

Forever Fruit

This is a method, without cooking, to turn assorted fruits into a sauce or dessert topping. It utilizes no-longer-fresh fruits, or bits of leftovers you don't know what to do with. Once you've established a Forever Fruit crock in the corner of your kitchen, you won't need any directions. But until you get the hang of it, you might start in this way.

In a ceramic or earthenware crock, combine 1 cup pineapple chunks and 1 cup sugar; cover them with vodka.

A week later, add 1 cup pitted sweet cherries, and enough vodka to cover all the fruit.

A week after that, add 1 cup peach or nectarine chunks and 1 cup sugar.

And a week after *that*, add some raisins and minced apple.

Stir the fruit with each addition, taste it for sweetness from time to time (and add sugar or not, accordingly), and see that the fruit stays covered with vodka (or whatever liquor you want to use).

Whenever you want a topping for a freshly made pudding, ice cream, or sherbet, drain the fruit as you scoop it out, put some more fresh fruit in—and you will have a liqueur of fruit forever.

INDEX

A

Almond
  plum tart, 84
  torte, nectarine, 110–111
  torte, peach, 110–111
Apples, 11–12. *See also*
    Applesauce
  blackberry sherbet, 134
  cake, simple, 108
  carambola stars, 28
  cheese soufflé, 60
  chocolate melba, 140–141
  crunch, 96
  fruited flan, 61
  fruited Indian pudding, 69
  green, Betty, 100
  hot candied, 154–155
  passion fruit cup, 37
  pecan delight, 64–65
  pecan torte, 110–111
  pie, 88
  tart, tart, 81
  watermelon bowl, 38–39

Applesauce
  cake, simple, 108
  foam, 49
  imperial, 156
Apricots, 12
  banana mousse, 35
  cheese pizza, 164
  meringue tart, 82–83
  mousse, chocolate, 46
  nut crumble, 99
  supreme, dried, 31
  supreme, fresh, 31
  tart, prune, 86
Avocados, 12
  fresh fig ambrosia, 29
  ice cream, 138–139
  mousse, pear, 35
  mousse, plum, 35

B

Baked banana, 159
Bananas, 12–13
  baked, 159
  cake, 118
  cheesecake, 104–105
  mousse, apricot, 35
  passion fruit cup, 37
  passion fruit ice, 124–125
  roll, fried, 160–161

tropical fruit macedoine, 36
  whip, strawberry, 32
Berries, 13. *See also* specific
    berries
  bread pudding, 67
  cheese tart, 87
  cobbler, 94
  cream, 56
  crush, 123
  ice cream, 138
  meringue tart, 82
  parfait, 30
  pear tart, 80
  rice pudding, 68
  shortcake, 116–117
  soufflé, 59
  tapioca, 53
  yogurt, frozen, 137
  yogurt tart, 90–91
Bilberries. *See* Blueberries
Black currant tart, 85
Blackberries, 13. *See also*
    Berries
  berry
    bread pudding, 67
    cheese tart, 87
    cobbler, 94
    cream, 56
    crush, 123
    ice cream, 138

meringue tart, 82
pear tart, 80
rice pudding, 68
tapioca, 53
cheesecake II, 104
frozen berry yogurt, 137
fruited flan, 61
pecan melba, 140–141
rainbow cream, 148
sherbet, apple, 134
Blueberries, 13. *See also*
    Berries
berry
    bread pudding, 67
    cheese tart, 87
    cobbler, 94
    cream, 56
    crush, 123
    ice cream, 138
    meringue tart, 82
    parfait, 30
    pear tart, 80
    rice pudding, 68
    tapioca, 53
cheesecake II, 104
coffeecake, 109
frozen berry yogurt, 137
fruited flan, 61
rainbow cream, 148

yogurt tart, 90–91
Bombe
    raspberry, 144–145
    strawberry, 144–145
Boysenberries. *See*
    Blackberries
Bread pudding, berry, 67
Brownies, raspberry, 114
Butter pastry, 74–75

C

Cake. *See also* Cheesecake
    apple pecan torte, 110–111
    banana, 118
    berry shortcake, 116–117
    blueberry coffeecake, 109
    fig torte, 112–113
    ginger pear, 107
    nectarine almond torte,
        110–111
    peach almond torte, 110–111
    peach shortcake, 116–117
    pineapple shortcake,
        116–117
    plum, 106
    prune torte, 112–113
    simple apple, 108
    simple applesauce, 108

strawberry shortcake,
    116–117
Cantaloupes, 19. *See also*
    Melons
    froth, 146
    melon cream, 43
    melon mold, 52
    melon sorbet, 128
    passion fruit ice, 124–125
    pineapple pot, 40
Carambolas, 13–14
    stars, 28
Casabas, 19. *See also* Melons
    pineapple pot, 40
Catawba peach soup, 157
Cheese. *See also* Cheesecake
    pizza, apricot, 164
    soufflé
        apple, 60
        cherry, 60
        nectarine, 60
    tart, berry, 87
Cheesecake
    banana, 104–105
    cherry, 104–105
    I, 103
    peach, 104–105
    pineapple, 104–105
    II, 104

Cherries, sour, 14
  pie, 89
Cherries, sweet, 14
  Charlotte, 54–55
  cheese soufflé, 60
  cheesecake, 104–105
  freeze, chocolate, 143
  parfait, 30
  rice pudding, 68
  sorbet, 130–131
  yogurt tart, 90–91
Chocolate
  apricot mousse, 46
  cherry freeze, 143
  kiwi mousse, 46–47
  melba, apple, 140–141
  orange freeze, 143
  peach mousse, 46–47
  persimmon mousse, 46–47
  raspberry freeze, 143
  tangerine freeze, 142
Citrus fruits, 14–15. *See also*
      specific fruits
Cobbler
  berry, 94
  gooseberry, 92–93
  mulberry, 92–93
  rhubarb, 92–93
Coffeecake, blueberry, 109

Cranberries, 13. *See also*
      Berries
  crumble, 97
  frost, 126–127
  papaya whip, 32–33
Crumble
  apricot nut, 99
  cranberry, 97
  plum nut, 99
  rhubarb, 98
  strawberry rhubarb, 98
Crust. *See also* Pastry; Shell
  about, 72
  half-and-half, 74–75
Currants, 13
  black, tart, 85
  Muckleshoot raspberry
      pudding, 158
  red, crush, 123
Custard, double strawberry, 62

D

Dates
  apple crunch, 96
  dried apricot supreme, 31
  fresh apricot supreme, 31
Dewberries. *See* Blackberries
Double strawberry custard, 62
Dried apricot supreme, 31

F

Figs, 15
  ambrosia, fresh, 29
  torte, 112–113
Flan, fruited, 61
Fool
  gooseberry, 44–45
  guava, 44–45
  mango, 44–45
  nectarine, 44–45
  peach, 44–45
  pineapple, 44–45
Foolproof pastry, 73
Forever fruit, 166
Fresh apricot supreme, 31
Fried banana roll, 160–161
Fritters 'n fruit, 162–163
Frozen berry yogurt, 137
Frozen oranges, 147
Frozen peach yogurt, 137
Fruit, 6–7. *See also* specific
      fruits
  day-old, 10–11
  forever, 166
  fresh, serving ideas, 26–27
  fritters 'n, 162–163
  fruited flan, 61
  fruited Indian pudding, 69
  local, 10

over-ripe, 10–11, 102
peeling, 23
preventing discoloring, 24
sauce, 165
storage, 10
Fruited flan, 61
Fruited Indian pudding, 69

G

Garnishes, 58
Ginger pear cake, 107
Gooseberries, 13. *See also* ,
    Berries
  cobbler, 92–93
  fool, 44–45
  sticks, 153
Graham cracker shell, 76
Grapefruits, 14–15
  fruited flan, 61
  sherbet, 135
  snow, 48
Grapes, 15–16
  papaya mold, 51
  passion fruit cup, 37
  pineapple pot, 40
Green apple Betty, 100
Green papaya sherbet, 133
Green pear sherbet, 133

Guavas, 16–17
  fool, 44–45
  pomegranate sorbet, 129
  sorbet, 130–131
  tart, 78
  tropical fruit ice cream,
    138–139
  whip, 34

H

Half-and-half crust, 74
Honeydew melons, 19. *See
    also* Melons
  melon sorbet, 128
  passion fruit ice, 124–125
  pineapple pot, 40
Hot candied apples, 154–155
Huckleberries. *See*
    Blueberries

I

Ice, 120–121. *See also* Ice
    cream; Sherbet; Sorbet
  berry crush, 123
  cranberry frost, 126–127
  passion fruit, 124–125
  red currant crush, 123
  scarlet ambrosia, 122

Ice cream, 120–121. *See also*
    Ice; Sherbet; Sorbet
  apple chocolate melba,
    140–141
  avocado, 138–139
  berry, 138
  blackberry pecan melba,
    140–141
  chocolate
    cherry freeze, 143
    orange freeze, 143
    raspberry freeze, 143
    tangerine freeze, 142
  peach, 138–139
  raspberry walnut melba, 140
  strawberry pistachio melba,
    140
  tropical fruit, 138–139
Imperial applesauce, 156
Indian pudding, fruited, 69

K

Kiwis, 17
  mousse, chocolate, 46–47
  sorbet, 130–131
Kumquats, 17–18
  watermelon bowl, 38–39

L

Lemons, 14–15
  mint pears, 152
Limes, 14–15
  guava whip, 34
  mango whip, 34
  pear whip, 34
Lingonberries. *See*
      Cranberries
Loganberries. *See*
      Blackberries
Lychees, watermelon bowl,
      38–39

M

Macaroon peaches, 70
Mandarin oranges, 14–15
Mangoes, 18
  fool, 44–45
  pudding, 66
  sorbet, 128
  tropical fruit ice cream,
      138–139
  tropical fruit macedoine, 36
  whip, 34
Melons, 19. *See also* specific
      melons
  cream, 43

mold, 52
sorbet, 128
Meringue tart
  apricot, 82–83
  berry, 82
  nectarine, 82–83
  peach, 82–83
Mint pears, 152
Mousse
  apricot banana, 35
  chocolate
    apricot, 46
    kiwi, 46–47
    peach, 46–47
    persimmon, 46–47
  pear avocado, 35
  plum avocado, 35
Muckleshoot raspberry
      pudding, 158
Mulberries, 13. *See also*
      Berries
  berry cream, 56
  cobbler, 92–93

N

Nectarines, 20. *See also*
      Peaches
  almond torte, 110–111
  cheese soufflé, 60

fool, 44–45
fruited flan, 61
fruited Indian pudding, 69
meringue tart, 82–83
pie, 88
Nut
  crumble, apricot, 99
  crumble, plum, 99
  pastry shell, 77

O

Oranges, 14–15
  cantaloupe froth, 146
  dried apricot supreme, 31
  freeze, chocolate, 143
  frozen, 147
  fruit sauce, 165
  fruited flan, 61
  peach froth, 146
  rainbow cream, 148
  sherbet, 132
  sponge, 63
  tapioca, 53

P

Papayas, 19–20
  green, sherbet, 133
  mold, 51
  pudding, 66

tropical fruit macedoine, 36
whip, cranberry, 32–33
Parfait
  berry, 30
  cherry, 30
  peach, 30
Passion fruit, 20
  cup, 37
  ice, 124–125
  tropical fruit ice cream,
    138–139
Pastry. *See also* Crust; Shell
  butter, 74–75
  foolproof, 73
  shell, nut, 77
Peaches, 20. *See also*
    Nectarines
  almond torte, 110–111
  Charlotte, 54–55
  cheesecake, 104–105
  crisp, 95
  foam, 49
  fool, 44–45
  froth, 146
  fruited flan, 61
  fruited Indian pudding, 69
  ice cream, 138–139
  macaroon, 70

meringue tart, 82–83
mousse, chocolate, 46–47
parfait, 30
pie, 88
shortcake, 116–117
soup, Catawba, 157
tapioca, 53
yogurt, frozen, 137
yogurt tart, 90–91
Pears, 20–21
  avocado mousse, 35
  cake, ginger, 107
  foam, 49
  fruited flan, 61
  green, sherbet, 133
  mint, 152
  rainbow cream, 148
  sorbet, 128
  soufflé, 59
  tart, berry, 80
  vanilla, 151
  whip, 34
Pecan
  delight, apple, 64–65
  melba, blackberry, 140–141
  torte, apple, 110–111
Persimmons, 21
  mousse, chocolate, 46–47

pudding, 66
tart, 79
Pie
  apple, 88
  nectarine, 88
  peach, 88
  sour cherry, 89
Pineapples, 21–22
  Charlotte, 54–55
  cheesecake, 104–105
  fool, 44–45
  pot, 40
  shortcake, 116–117
  sponge, 63
  squares, 115
  tropical fruit macedoine, 36
Pistachio melba, strawberry,
    140
Pizza, apricot cheese, 164
Plums, 22
  avocado mousse, 35
  cake, 106
  delight, fresh, 64–65
  nut crumble, 99
  pudding, 66
  tart, almond, 84
Pomegranates, sorbet, guava,
    129

Prunes, 22
  apricot tart, 86
  torte, 112–113
Pudding
  berry bread, 67
  berry rice, 68
  cherry rice, 68
  fruited Indian, 69
  mango, 66
  Muckleshoot raspberry, 158
  papaya, 66
  persimmon, 66
  plum, 66
  tapioca
    berry, 53
    orange, 53
    peach, 53

Q

Quick light graham cracker
        shell, 76
Quinces, 22
  sherbet, 136

R

Rainbow cream, 148

Raisins
  fruited Indian pudding, 69
  imperial applesauce, 156
Raspberries, 13. *See also*
        Berries
berry
    bread pudding, 67
    cheese tart, 87
    cobbler, 94
    cream, 56
    crush, 123
    ice cream, 138
    meringue tart, 82
    parfait, 30
    pear tart, 80
    rice pudding, 68
    tapioca, 53
    yogurt tart, 90–91
  bombe, 144–145
  brownies, 114
  cheesecake II, 104
  freeze, chocolate, 143
  frozen berry yogurt, 137
  fruited flan, 61
  pineapple pot, 40
  pudding, Muckleshoot, 158
  rainbow cream, 148
  scarlet ambrosia, 122

    sherbet, 132
    vanilla pears, 151
    walnut melba, 140
    watermelon bowl, 38–39
    watermelon froth, 146
Red currant crush, 123
Rhubarb, 23
  cobbler, 92–93
  crumble, 98
    strawberry, 98
  delight, 50
Rice pudding
  berry, 68
  cherry, 68

S

Sauce
  forever fruit, 166
  fruit, 165
Scarlet ambrosia, 122
Shell. *See also* Crust; Pastry
  graham cracker, 76
  nut pastry, 77
  quick light graham cracker,
        76
Sherbet, 120–121. *See also*
        Ice; Ice cream; Sorbet
  apple blackberry, 134
  cantaloupe froth, 146

grapefruit, 135
green papaya, 133
green pear, 133
orange, 132
peach froth, 146
quince, 136
rainbow cream, 148
raspberry, 132
raspberry bombe, 144–145
strawberry bombe, 144–145
watermelon froth, 146
Shortcake
  berry, 116–117
  peach, 116–117
  pineapple, 116–117
  strawberry, 116–117
Simple apple cake, 108
Simple applesauce cake, 108
Sorbet, 120–121. *See also* Ice;
    Ice cream; Sherbet
  cherry, 130–131
  guava, 130–131
  guava pomegranate, 129
  kiwi, 130–131
  mango, 128
  melon, 128
  pear, 128
  watermelon, 130–131

Soufflé
  apple cheese, 60
  berry, 59
  cherry cheese, 60
  nectarine cheese, 60
  pear, 59
Soup, Catawba peach, 157
Sour cherry pie, 89
Star fruit. *See* Carambolas
Strawberries, 23. *See also*
    Berries
  banana whip, 32
  berry
    ice cream, 138
    meringue tart, 82
    parfait, 30
    tapioca, 53
    yogurt tart, 90–91
  bombe, 144–145
  cheesecake II, 104
  custard, double, 62
  frozen berry yogurt, 137
  fruited flan, 61
  pistachio melba, 140
  rhubarb crumble, 98
  scarlet ambrosia, 122
  shortcake, 116–117
Sugar, 7

T
Tangelos, 14–15
Tangerines, 14–15
  freeze, chocolate, 142
  fresh apricot supreme, 31
  fruited flan, 61
  watermelon bowl, 38–39
Tapioca
  berry, 53
  orange, 53
  peach, 53
Tart
  almond plum, 84
  apricot meringue, 82–83
  berry
    cheese, 87
    meringue, 82
    pear, 80
    yogurt, 90–91
  black currant, 85
  blueberry yogurt, 90–91
  cherry yogurt, 90–91
  guava, 78
  nectarine meringue, 82–83
  peach meringue, 82–83
  peach yogurt, 90–91
  persimmon, 79
  prune apricot, 86

tart apple, 81
Tart apple tart, 81
Torte. *See also* Cake
  apple pecan, 110–111
  fig, 112–113
  nectarine almond, 110–111
  peach almond, 110–111
  prune, 112–113
Tropical fruit ice cream,
     138–139
Tropical fruit macedoine, 36

V

Vanilla pears, 151

W

Walnut melba, raspberry, 140
Watermelons, 19. *See also*
     Melons
  bowl, 38–39
  froth, 146
  melon mold, 52
  pineapple pot, 40
  sorbet, 130–131
Whip
  cranberry papaya, 32–33
  guava, 34
  mango, 34

pear, 34
  strawberry banana, 32
Whipping
  cream, 42
  egg whites, 42
Whortleberries. *See*
     Blueberries

Y

Yogurt
  frozen berry, 137
  frozen peach, 137
  tart
    berry, 90–91
    blueberry, 90–91
    cherry, 90–91
    peach, 90–91